"Hands down the best, most helpful book on perfectionism I've ever encountered. A must-read for anyone looking to escape the cage of self-imposed perfectionistic expectations and behaviors."

—**Jill A. Stoddard, PhD**, author of *Be Mighty*, coauthor of *The Big Book of ACT Metaphors*, and cohost of the *Psychologists Off the Clock* podcast

"The irony of this book is that it is a perfect workbook to help you reduce your struggle with perfectionism. Jennifer Kemp's gentle voice feels like a warm, compassionate blanket that is there to soothe you and help you to create a kinder relationship with yourself."

—**Janina Scarlet, PhD**, award-winning author of *Superhero Therapy*

"Jennifer Kemp has created a wonderful workbook for those struggling with clinical perfectionism. Using skills from acceptance and commitment therapy (ACT), you can learn to use your perfectionism when it works for you, and not be held back by it when it tries to slow you down. Practicing what is in this book can improve your life."

—**Michael Twohig, PhD**, professor at Utah State University, and coauthor of *The Anxious Perfectionist*

"In *The ACT Workbook for Perfectionism*, Jennifer Kemp generously offers her expertise alongside her lived experience to lead the reader through a tough but potentially life-changing journey. It *empowers* readers with the latest scientific approaches for understanding and unwinding the grip of perfectionism, and *inspires* readers with relatable stories and actionable exercises. Anyone who finds themselves seeing what's 'best' as the only acceptable way forward should pick up this book as a first step in building *their* best, imperfect life."

—**Emily K. Sandoz, PhD**, endowed professor of social sciences, and graduate coordinator at University of Louisiana at Lafayette

"Jennifer Kemp is not perfect, and that makes this book perfect. Her voice is so relatable and honest, it's like a conversation. Drawing on personal and client experience, the book is warm and accessible, whilst also being structured, interactive, and academically impressive. Kemp uses the latest science of behavior change, delivered in an engaging series of exercises and readings, to help you change your own perfectionist habits."

—**David Gillanders**, head of clinical and health psychology at the University of Edinburgh

"At last, a workbook for perfectionists that is practical, heartfelt, and based on the science of ACT. It is packed with practical tools, readings, exercises, and ideas for change. This is a wonderful resource for helping you do the things that really matter, and getting your demanding, critical self-talk out of the driver's seat. It will help you create a life you care about."

—**Louise Hayes, PhD**, clinical psychologist; and coauthor of *The Thriving Adolescent*; *Your Life, Your Way*; and *Get Out of Your Mind and Into Your Life for Teens*

"Perfectionism can lead to that frozen and self-critical place where individuals feel overwhelmed and unable to move forward. Jennifer Kemp has offered an alternative to this suffering in *The ACT Workbook for Perfectionism*. She guides readers through a process that is both helpful and compassionate. A fantastic resource for self-guided work in letting go and embracing the imperfect! She has developed this book to support healthy engagement in life."

—**Robyn D. Walser, PhD**, licensed clinical psychologist; author of *The Heart of ACT*; and coauthor of *Learning ACT*, *The Mindful Couple*, *Acceptance and Commitment Therapy for the Treatment of Post-Traumatic Stress Disorder and Trauma-Related Problems*, and *The ACT Workbook for Anger*

"Do you ever feel trapped in the struggle for perfection? Then this book is for you. Not only is it packed with practical and manageable suggestions on how to take small, imperfect steps toward building a life you love. It teaches you how to no longer be held back by fear of failure, criticism, or unhelpful high standards. I truly love this book. And I am sure you will too."

—**Rikke Kjelgaard**, licensed psychologist, author, and expert in ACT

The
ACT Workbook
for Perfectionism

Build Your Best *(Imperfect)* Life Using
Powerful Acceptance and Commitment Therapy
and Self-Compassion Skills

Jennifer Kemp, MPsych

New Harbinger Publications, Inc.

Distributed in Canada by Raincoast Books

NEW HARBINGER PUBLICATIONS is a registered trademark of New Harbinger Publications, Inc.

Cover design by Sara Christain

Acquired by Tesilya Hanauer

FSC
www.fsc.org
MIX
Paper from
responsible sources
FSC® C011935

Library of Congress Cataloging-in-Publication Data

Names: Kemp, Jennifer (Psychologist), author.
Title: The ACT workbook for perfectionism : build your best (imperfect) life using powerful acceptance & commitment therapy and self-compassion skills / Jennifer Kemp, MPsych.
Description: Oakland, CA : New Harbinger Publications, [2021] | Includes bibliographical references.
Identifiers: LCCN 2021024778 | ISBN 9781684038077 (trade paperback)
Subjects: LCSH: Perfectionism (Personality trait) | Acceptance and commitment therapy.
Classification: LCC RC569.5.P45 K46 2021 | DDC 616.89/1425--dc23
LC record available at https://lccn.loc.gov/2021024778

Printed in the United States of America

23   22

10   9   8   7   6   5   4   3   2

To Maggie, Lachlan, and Paris—thank you for the hugs.

Contents

Foreword

I love this advice: "Everything good comes from patterns of practice, rather than any single great act. Another piece of every important practice has been falling. Learning to walk involves falling. Learning to be a partner, teacher, parent, has involved *a lot* of falling. I have learned to let falling be a part of my practice. People unwilling to fall do not get to know new and difficult things." When my daughter started college, my good friend and mentor Kelly Wilson wrote this to her.

By refusing to fall, perfectionism steals our opportunity to practice falling and the chance to learn from it. Our perfectionist minds are stealthy and convincing, promising excellence, security, and invulnerability—if only we get it right. They tell us that to be perfect equals safety; that when we arrive at "perfect" we will have truly accomplished. They promise that if we work our hardest and do all things perfectly, or if we avoid doing them entirely to protect against negative evaluation or failure, we won't ever have to feel things like shame, unworthiness, incompetence. For some, that story is so compelling we may even feel that if we can't live a perfect life, then maybe it isn't worth it to be alive.

All of these are lies. Our perfectionist minds keep moving the finish line over and over, farther and farther away. No matter how hard we try—no matter how many other parts of our lives we sacrifice at the altar of perfection—we are never done and we are never, ever enough. If we leave our perfectionism unexamined, we may be left with a life full of regrets. Dear reader, here is my wish for you: Don't let this be you. May you allow this book to be the fulcrum point on which your life begins to shift.

If you have this book in your hands and are reading these words, welcome. You belong here. You are one of us who strives for excellence in ways that are sometimes deeply unhelpful and downright harmful. You say: *But I need my perfectionism; that critical voice in my head is essential to my success.* And indeed, when we get things right that perfectionist piece of us is, for just a moment, satisfied. But what if there is another way to live, one in which you *choose* a more balanced life that harnesses your perfectionism more effectively? What if that life could touch a deeper sense of meaning, and purpose, and connection? What if you could experience a sense of wholeness, of gratitude for being in the world?

You are in luck! You are about to embark on an adventure that will help you crack open a different sort of life, one that feels expansive, and vital, and risky, and scary. As this book's author Jennifer Kemp puts it, this life involves "glorious messiness." She walks with you on a path that involves small, faltering, imperfect steps that *welcomes* falling. Take her advice: work the exercises in each chapter, dog-ear pages, write notes, underline passages. Follow her encouragement to learn how to use your perfectionism in effective, strategic, and life-expansive ways. Allow her to gently introduce you to a practice of self-kindness where there has been harsh self-criticism. Her only small requirement is that you cultivate a practice of curiosity and openness to learning—imperfectly.

I hope you do not use this book as part of your striving to "live a perfect life." Psychotherapist Carl Rogers said that what makes a good life is not *achievement;* rather, it is the process and direction of living "when there is psychological freedom to move in any direction" (Rogers 1961). Approaching your *process* of perfectionism with awareness and sensitivity, guided by Jennifer Kemp's gentle and clear instruction, will help you to strengthen elements that serve you well and to discard those that get in your way. If you take her up on this invitation, you will learn to let go of "perfect," practice falling, and take spectacular risks of imperfection in order to make space and time for living with vitality and joy.

Welcome. The only way we learn to rise is through falling. May you rise into a life that you will cherish.

—Lisa W. Coyne, PhD

The Tyranny of Perfectionism

If I waited for perfection, I would never write a word.

—Margaret Atwood

Do you set ambitious standards for yourself?

Since you've picked up this book on perfectionism, I'm betting that you do—and you probably wouldn't have it any other way. Striving for excellence may have given you some outstanding results: high grades, a well-paid job, or maybe, excellence in sporting or artistic fields. If this is the case, at some point, your perfectionism was working for you and you have flourished as a result. This is *helpful perfectionism,* where your perfectionistic habits help you be successful and achieve your goals, and where you enjoy working hard in this way.

It is also likely that, at times, perfectionism isn't entirely working for your benefit. You may be having difficulty trying new things or taking risks because you fear failing or looking stupid. Perhaps you have trouble putting plans into action because you worry about making mistakes, put things off until the last minute, or get bogged down with details in ways that cause you a lot of added stress. You might find it difficult to try new things and make decisions. You may present a perfect image to the world, yet feel anxious and tense, critical of yourself, and full of self-doubt. It can seem that no matter what you achieve, you are never good enough.

This is *unhelpful perfectionism,* and it comes at a great cost to your well-being. What may have started as helpful habits has become something much more destructive. Unhelpful perfectionism is linked to common psychological problems including depression, anxiety, and body-image problems. The habits can interfere with healthy eating and exercise too. Unhelpful perfectionism can undermine your goals in life, leaving you feeling like you are floundering, worn out, exhausted, or frozen—unable to move toward the things that really matter to you.

If you struggle with unhelpful perfectionism, this book is for you. Together, we'll focus on this "dark side" of perfectionism, what drives such unhelpful behaviors, why they persist even though they are causing you problems, and how you can change them into something that works better for you. Even if you have been struggling with these problems for a long time, it is possible to change things for the better, *without lowering your standards, being lazy, or doing poor work.* You may only need to dial back your perfectionism by 10 percent to achieve a more fulfilling and productive life. I've written this book to help you learn how to be *much more than "perfect"*—how to be your whole self, living a full and meaningful life that you've created, without losing the things that are important to you such as your personal standards and your drive to achieve.

Breaking Free from Perfectionism

I know what it feels like to struggle with perfectionism. Even as a child, I always needed to get things right. I often avoided things I couldn't do well. At times, I've experienced anxiety that's left me breathless, shaking, and in floods of tears. I've struggled to accept feedback without being defensive. Sometimes I've felt devastated for days. I've been paralyzed with indecision because I couldn't risk making the wrong choice. I've experienced the dark alleyways of depression and struggled to get out of bed when things have gone wrong.

Yet I only fully realized just how much I struggled with perfectionism when I was in my late thirties. I had started studying clinical psychology and attended a one-day seminar about perfectionism with Professor Tracey Wade. At the start of the day, she played the song "Never Good Enough" by Rachel Ferguson and my eyes immediately swelled with tears. During that day, so much fell into place for me. Many of the problems I'd been having in my life were tied to one consistent theme: perfectionism. I'd known I was "a bit perfectionistic," but I hadn't realized how this linked together very painful problems I'd been facing all these years.

It was then that I started the journey toward better managing my perfectionism. Despite seeing several therapists over the years, no one had ever tried to address my perfectionism. Everyone had focused on the specific issues I was having at the time, without looking at the processes that tied things together. Perhaps, these therapists assumed perfectionism was part of my personality that I couldn't change.

I wrote down what I'd learned and took it to my psychologist. I believed that now I had the key to what was making me anxious and depressed. My psychologist at the time was using a Cognitive Behavior Therapy approach, and while I successfully changed some unhelpful habits, I had little success in permanently changing my thinking patterns. I started by focusing on finding the right balance of effort and reward. I was studying post-graduate psychology at the time, and with many competing demands (including young children), I stopped aiming for extremely high marks and instead aimed to hand things in when they were good enough. Finding this middle ground was challenging but rewarding, because I got to spend more time with my family and I still passed everything just fine.

It wasn't until the end of my post-graduate clinical psychology studies that I first discovered Acceptance and Commitment Therapy (ACT). To be honest, I couldn't see how to apply ACT to my own perfectionism at first, but little by little, as I began to learn the ACT processes better, I started to apply them to myself. I began to see my thoughts for what they were—just thoughts—and found I did not have to react in the same ways. I began to recognize and make room for some of the uncomfortable feelings that my perfectionism gave me and started to take steps toward what was important to me, even though I might risk failing.

Since finishing my studies, I've been fortunate to have many clients who have struggled with perfectionism and I've been able to use ACT with everyone, finding the tools and strategies helpful with a wide range of perfectionistic patterns. I've also had plenty of opportunities to address my own unhelpful perfectionistic habits along the way, such as worrying that my clients aren't improving fast enough (and assuming it must be my fault) and believing that I should be able to help everyone *all the time* (Deutsch 1984, Ellis 2003). I have also learned a lot from my clients about how to manage perfectionistic self-criticism.

This has been a long road for me. The most recent (and probably not last) piece of the puzzle fell into place when, in 2017, in a workshop run by my friend Dr. David Gillanders, I appreciated the importance of self-compassion. In this workshop I developed self-compassion for my own self-criticism for the first time and began to understand the good intentions hidden beneath my own self-critical voice. This activity helped my self-compassion grow—in later chapters you will try this for yourself. Since then, I've been able to take greater risks and experience greater satisfaction in my life.

It's taken me years to find a way to make my perfectionism function better for me, and although I would never claim to be done with this work, I have found ways to live a life I love rather than one that's constrained by my own perfectionistic rules. While I can still fall into perfectionistic traps, overall, I've learned to harness my perfectionism, welcome it as a (mostly) positive and helpful pressure, and use it as a force for good. It is my sincere hope that I can help you achieve this too.

About This Book

This book applies the knowledge and framework provided by behavioral science to understand unhelpful perfectionism and guide you to create positive changes in your life. It will help you to:

- Understand your own unique experience of perfectionism, how it influences the way you approach goals in your life, and how it can be transformed into something more useful.

- See the extent of the problems that perfectionism creates for you, including issues such as depression and anxiety, as well as difficulties with work, study, or relationships.

- Identify the fears that drive perfectionism and develop more helpful ways to respond to these fears.

- Describe what is important to you *beyond perfection* and apply clear steps so you can create a fulfilling and satisfying future.

- Be kinder, more encouraging, and more compassionate with yourself now and into the future, while still achieving excellence.

Through this book you'll make two crucial changes that will help you to manage your perfectionism better. You'll become more *flexible* by applying key skills and techniques from Acceptance and Commitment Therapy (ACT) and more *compassionate* toward yourself by applying the framework and skills of Compassion-Focused Therapy (CFT). To help you achieve this, I've chosen strategies and techniques that I've found useful and that my clients have found useful too. I've illustrated how it is possible to transform your perfectionism into something rightsized for your life using my own stories and those of the people I've worked with. I hope you can benefit from these experiences as you work through this book. In addition, there are also a host of materials available for download at the website for this book: http://www.newharbinger.com/48077. (See the very back of this book for more details.)

Becoming More Flexible

Pronounced as one word, "ACT" (Acceptance and Commitment Therapy) is one of several therapies that have further developed the ideas of Behaviorism and Cognitive Behavior Therapy (CBT) in what is called the "third wave" of CBT. ACT is a rapidly growing and scientifically based therapy with over three hundred randomized controlled trials demonstrating its effectiveness for a wide range of mental and physical health problems.

ACT is a therapeutic approach that is not designed to treat a specific mental health disorder. Rather, it addresses the unhelpful psychological processes that drive the problems people face in everyday life. The principles of ACT seem to apply in almost any situation—individually, in groups, workplaces, and communities—and it may even help guide how to address bigger global challenges, such as health and environmental crises. ACT can help any individual or group build the capabilities they need to be psychologically healthy. These capabilities are collectively known as *psychological flexibility*.

In his recent book *A Liberated Mind,* Dr. Steven Hayes describes psychological flexibility as "the ability to feel and think with openness, to attend voluntarily to your experience of the present moment, and to move your life in directions that are important to you, building habits that allow you to live life in accordance with your values and aspirations" (Hayes 2019, 5). Psychological *inflexibility* appears to be a core process in unhelpful perfectionism (Lundh 2004, Ong et al. 2019, Santanello and Gardner 2007), and recent research has shown that increasing psychological flexibility using ACT can help alleviate the problematic aspects of perfectionism (Ong et al. 2019). In this book, you will explore how to apply ACT skills to transform your unhelpful perfectionistic behaviors into more helpful choices.

Enhancing Your Self-Compassion

I suspect you tend to be hard on yourself. Human brains have an amazing ability to solve problems, something that has been extraordinarily useful for us as a species, but also left us prone to worrying, rumination, self-criticism, and shame. Learning to become more compassionate toward yourself in the presence of difficult and worrying experiences will help you unlock important skills that can help you with the many different challenges you'll face in life.

Compassion-Focused Therapy (CFT) is an innovative approach that originated in the United Kingdom from the work of the clinical psychologist Dr. Paul Gilbert. It looks at human behavior and the human mind from an evolutionary perspective, integrating techniques from both Eastern and Western traditions such as mindfulness and behaviorism, neuroscience, and attachment theory (Kolts 2016, Welford 2016). CFT aims to help people find compassionate ways to approach challenging and uncomfortable emotions and help people feel safe, secure, and confident in tackling problems in their lives. CFT is built on the understanding that self-compassion can be learned and practiced. Research supporting CFT is rapidly growing, with one recent study linking higher self-compassion with lower levels of unhelpful perfectionism (Ong et al. 2019). In this book, you are going to learn how to build greater self-compassion and apply these skills to tackle the self-criticism and shame that forms a key part of unhelpful perfectionism.

Reading Tips for Maximum Benefit

Work through this book from beginning to end. This book is designed to be read from start to finish, with each chapter building on the last to create a roadmap for positive change. Beginning with an exploration of how perfectionism affects your life today, the book provides small and achievable tasks that build into tangible steps to improve your life. You'll define what you really want to change, create a rich picture of a future life that will motivate and inspire you, and develop acceptance and self-compassion skills. The final chapters focus on taking meaningful steps toward change and getting back on track when things go wrong.

Take your time. It is likely that you've developed your perfectionistic habits over a long time. Likewise, changing habits takes time and repeated practice. It may take a week or more to complete each chapter and its activities. If you want to read each chapter in full first, this is okay, but please then go back and complete the activities before moving on to the next chapter.

Make this book your own. Do not treat this workbook like a precious object that needs to be kept pristine or perfectly clean! Write your responses to the questions straight into the book, take notes in the margins, and <u>underline</u> key points. This will not only help you deepen your learning but will also help you find what you need if you come back later to reread sections. Coffee stains, folded corners, and even bending the book backward are all signs that you are engaged with the content. Making a mess is also a small step toward not needing things to be so perfect, so go ahead, make a mess here, knowing it is also valuable practice. Have fun with it!

Attempt all the activities. Unhelpful perfectionism can interfere with completing challenging activities and trying new things. An interesting recent study found that perfectionists tend to procrastinate on homework assignments and those who score high in unhelpful perfectionism tend to start and complete fewer activities to improve their mood (Kobori, Dighton, and Hunter 2020). This is good to remember as you work through the book. Pay attention when you feel reluctant to do something because you can't do it *properly*. You may need to try doing it *imperfectly* instead.

Prepare to be uncomfortable at times. As you work through each chapter you may find some activities unusual, difficult, or even confusing. I vividly remember the first time I tried to do a mindfulness activity. My college lecturer sat us all in a circle and launched into a twenty-minute practice with no warning or explanation. At the time I was a stressed-out graduate student. My mind went into overdrive and I felt every restless ache and twinge in my body all at once. It was a lot to deal with, and it was some time before I tried mindfulness again. (Can you tell how upsetting I found it?) It would have helped me greatly if she'd given us more warning about what to expect and told us how long we would be doing the activity. Instead of sitting in a circle where people would see me fidget, we could have sat spaced apart, giving us privacy to deal with any discomfort.

For this reason, whenever there is a mindfulness activity in this book, please understand that any suggestions of timing are only recommendations. Be sure to find a quiet and private space. Move your body if you need to get more comfortable. If you are finding five minutes for a mindfulness activity to be too difficult, try just two minutes. If this is too uncomfortable, try one minute. *Any* practice is valuable, no matter how long. If your mind is particularly busy, then having a one-minute vacation from worrying or problem-solving can make a remarkable difference.

Be patient with yourself. You may benefit from rereading parts of this book or practicing activities several times to allow the learning to deepen. I know this may be at odds with your perfectionistic expectations! With a bit of practice, and starting with much shorter sessions, I now usually find mindfulness a rewarding and soothing activity, although not every time I practice it. Don't feel too disheartened if something doesn't work out well the first time. Most of the practical activities in this book work best if you practice them daily for a week or more, and they become easier over time too. To help you further, you'll find recordings of some activities at http://www.newharbinger.com/48077.

Practice makes…better, eventually. Remember that new habits need to be practiced in lots of different situations to become automatic. For this reason, I also encourage you to try out all the activities more than once. My goal is to help you achieve lasting, positive change, but I know from my own experience that this will take time. I continue to find myself falling into perfectionistic traps even today. Authoring this book has been demanding and required me to let go of my need for perfection, hence the inspiring quote from Margaret Atwood, a writer I greatly admire, at the beginning of this chapter. While it took me some time to get started, I didn't give up. I hope you won't give up either. Also, remember that old habits have a way of returning when you are under pressure or in periods of change or stress. This is a normal and natural part of the change process, and if this happens to you, you are not alone. Use this book as a guide to get back on track at any stage. You may also want to seek the help of a licensed therapist if things get too difficult.

Try to put new strategies into action straightaway. At the end of each chapter, there is a chance to deepen your learning and plan your small, imperfect steps toward change. I'm a behavioral therapist, so I always want to know what you will *do* differently because of what you've learned. *Thinking* about change will not make any difference to your problems—taking action is what counts. Planning your next steps at the end of each chapter will help you focus on small, helpful things you can do right away.

Activity: Choose Your Own Adventure

Before you set out on this adventure, it's always useful to think about where you want to go. Your preparation for change starts right now. In this first activity you will have an opportunity to think about what you would like to get out of reading this book. Read the following paragraphs through first, then find a quiet, peaceful place to complete this activity.

Start by closing your eyes or looking down toward the floor, placing your feet squarely on the ground and sitting up in your chair so that your back is straight and your head feels supported on your shoulders. Notice the feeling of your body resting on the chair, including all the parts of your body that are touching the chair. Notice how your feet are resting on the floor. Take three slow, deep breaths, and let your body sink into your space, feeling the support of the chair and the floor, holding you in place. Allow yourself to settle comfortably for a minute or two.

Consider the following questions. Allow any ideas to pass freely through your mind. Allow yourself a minute or two to consider each question in turn.

1.   What would you like to get out of working through this book?

2.   Think about how you are struggling with perfectionism right now. How would you like to change this?

3.   As you work through this book, how will you know that your perfectionism is improving? What positive changes might you notice in yourself? What differences might emerge in your life more broadly?

Take one further deep breath and allow a gentle smile to form across your face. In your own time, feel your feet resting on the floor and your body resting on the chair. Open your eyes. Then, in your own time, complete the questions below.

Simply write down your first ideas as they occur to you—there are no correct answers.

By reading this book, I would really like to learn:

1.   _____

2.   _____

3.   _____

Two aspects of my perfectionism that I'd like to change are:

1.   _____

2.   _____

I would know my perfectionism was not such a problem anymore if I could:

1. _____

2. _____

3. _____

You've taken a major step by picking up this book. My job is to show you how to make your life better and give you a pathway to achieve that. You can overcome unhelpful patterns, escape the tyranny of perfectionistic standards, and live a more fulfilling life. Let's get started.

CHAPTER 1

Are You Trapped in the Struggle for Perfection?

The most difficult times for many of us are the ones we give ourselves.

—Pema Chödrön, *When Things Fall Apart*

Many people think of perfectionism as a personality trait, something that affects you during your whole life. Yet, if you see perfectionism as part of your personality, it is difficult to change. I help people struggling with perfectionism who, like you, want to change their lives for the better. I watch people transform their unhelpful perfectionistic habits into new helpful patterns that lead to a more fulfilling life. To do this, I approach perfectionism as a set of behaviors that are learned, and therefore, something you can change.

Perfectionistic behaviors are learned and can be helpful (adaptive) or unhelpful (maladaptive) (Owens and Slade 2008, Slade and Owens 1998). Helpful perfectionistic behaviors support you in achieving goals, facing challenges, deepening relationships, and creating a fulfilling life. Unhelpful perfectionistic behaviors lead you to hide from the things that scare you or repeat destructive patterns that hurt you in the long run. In this book, you will explore your current habits and learn how to change unhelpful habits into new patterns that work better for you.

Many of my clients come to me because they feel anxious, worn out, demoralized, and unsatisfied with their life. Some have a life full of conflict, trauma, or stress. Others can't pinpoint any specific trigger, yet, they still feel disconnected, tense, or lonely. Each person has developed ways to cope with this; they drink, eat, don't eat, gamble, take painkillers, work hard, argue, smoke weed, withdraw, or harm themselves. They try to be perfect to avoid further pain or loss. These habits make sense when you look at what the behavior is trying to achieve (relief, safety, and an end to pain), but they also cause other problems.

Perfectionism is a pattern of behavior that, when changed, can help people live better lives and let go of unhealthy ways of coping. By changing your unhelpful perfectionistic habits into behaviors that are more helpful, you can build your confidence, achieve more, connect with others, and take risks that expand your life in positive ways. The first step is to figure out what perfectionism looks like for you.

The Five Processes of Perfectionism

Looking at perfectionism as a set of five unhelpful processes is a pragmatic approach that shifts the focus from there being something wrong with you to being stuck with unhelpful habits that can be changed. There are five behavior patterns that are common among people with unhelpful perfectionism. The first two processes seem to drive unhelpful habits: setting standards for yourself that are excessive and rigid and having an intense fear of failure. The second two describe the way you respond to the first: by criticizing yourself when you don't meet your own ideals and by avoiding things to reduce your fear. The final process recognizes the broader issues that avoidance and self-criticism can cause in your life.

Check any of these processes that might apply to you:

☐ Setting extremely ambitious, inflexible benchmarks for your performance and tending to raise these standards over time

☐ Intensely fearing failure or mistakes, including social mistakes and not being liked

☐ Persistent, demoralizing self-criticism and never feeling good enough because you can never meet your criterion for success

☐ Avoiding certain situations, places, or people so you can avoid feelings of failure and self-criticism

☐ Bigger problems appearing in your life because of this avoidance

Over the coming pages, we'll look at each of these in more detail. Each section includes stories that illustrate the processes. As you read them, notice any aspects that resonate for you and underline these passages. We'll come back to these points at the end of the section.

Excessively High and Inflexible Standards

Do you set ambitious targets for your performance and treat these standards as if they are unbreakable rules? Do you discount your goals as "too easy" once you achieve them and raise the bar for next time? If so, your goals (and the feelings of satisfaction that come from achieving them) will always be just out of reach. You'll end up feeling like you are failing even as you achieve a great deal. You may even want to give up altogether, knowing that you won't be happy, whatever you do. This problem becomes bigger if you also set rigid standards for colleagues, friends, or family members. People may feel like they are never good enough for you, leading to tension and even the breakdown of important relationships (Trub et al. 2018).

> *Jonas worked as a team leader for a large manufacturer. He had two young children with his wife, Maree, who also works part-time. On Fridays, Jonas's parents picked up the kids from day care and brought them home after dinner. Every week, when Jonas got home from work, he felt immediately on edge. He prided himself on keeping a neat and organized home and worried what his parents would think about the mess. So, from the moment he walked in the door, Jonas started tidying and cleaning. This caused tension with Maree, who felt criticized and pressured. By the time the kids got home, both Jonas and Maree were frustrated and on edge, and Jonas had withdrawn into his study for the rest of the night. While he felt disappointed in himself as a father, Jonas didn't know how to stop this pattern from happening each week.*

When you set unreasonably high and inflexible expectations of yourself, it causes significant stress for yourself and others. Underline any aspects of Jonas's story that are like your own experience. You will explore the standards you set for yourself later in this chapter.

Fear of Failure

Pervasive fear of failing is at the heart of unhelpful perfectionism and seems to drive most unhelpful behaviors. "Failure" can be a wide range of things such as making a mistake, being socially awkward, not being liked or loved enough, or not earning enough money. Fear of failure is generally more intense when other people might see you fail.

> *Natalie worked as a draftsperson in a construction firm. She had originally wanted to be an architect, but she found the program to be stressful and had difficulty handing in her assignments. Eventually, she withdrew and completed a drafting certificate. Believing she was not a good learner, Natalie avoided doing further study. Natalie's daily job was to draw up construction plans. She needed to be fast and exact to avoid delays on-site. Natalie found the rapid pace of the work to be stressful. She worried about making a mistake that would cause problems on-site, so she*

checked all her work several times to make sure it was correct. As a result, Natalie had difficulty getting everything done. When her boss asked her to work faster, Natalie berated herself as "a failure" and "hopeless." Finding it difficult to increase her speed, Natalie worked late into the evenings and left each night feeling drained and demoralized, not knowing how to make things better.

Natalie works harder and harder to avoid making mistakes and avoids any situation where she might fail. Underline any parts of Natalie's story that ring true for you. You will explore your fear of failure in greater detail in Chapter 2.

Relentless Self-Criticism

Self-criticism is one of the most invasive and debilitating perfectionistic behaviors and leaves you feeling hopeless, worthless, and useless. Self-critical thoughts can be mean and hurt deeply. It's shocking just how nasty we can be to ourselves. Your self-critical thoughts might criticize what you do ("I never do anything right"), predict a bad future ("I will never succeed"), or criticize you as a person ("I am so useless," "I am a loser," or "I'll never be good enough"). Persistently berating yourself in this way will erode your self-confidence over time.

Sofia was a twenty-year-old college student who was studying psychology while working part-time in a café. Concerned about fitting in on campus, Sofia worried that people would think she was unattractive and wouldn't like her. Every day, Sofia put a lot of effort into her appearance, making sure her outfit was both cool and casual; her makeup was flawless yet natural, and devising the perfect yet messy hairstyle. In class, Sofia worked hard to make sure she got good grades because, if she didn't, she would privately call herself "stupid," "hopeless," and a "complete failure." Even though to the outside world her life looked perfect, Sofia struggled to make friends. Sofia felt devastated when she heard other students whispering sarcastically that she was "always so perfect." Beneath her polished facade, Sofia felt crushed by the pressure of maintaining the appearance of a perfect life. Deep down, she believed that she would never be good enough to have the close friendships she longed for.

Sofia harshly criticizes herself every day, finding that trying to be perfect is causing her more problems than it solves. Underline any part of this story that seems familiar to you. In later chapters, you will explore your self-criticism and learn how to calm your self-critical voice using self-compassion.

Unhelpful Avoidance

Avoiding things that make you feel uncomfortable makes perfect sense. Naturally, you would prefer to avoid failing, especially if you know you will severely criticize yourself if you do. Some people avoid failure by working harder, such as repeatedly checking their work, working too much, or looking for reassurance. Others avoid the potential for failure by procrastinating, taking a safer option, or avoiding the task altogether. Avoiding things in these ways can narrow your options and make life less fulfilling.

Now in his forties, Sam had found his weight gradually increasing over the years. Despite going on many different diets and exercise plans and sometimes losing a lot of weight, Sam hadn't been able to sustain the weight loss. When Sam went to the gym, he still tried to work out like he used to when he was younger and fitter, but ended up sore for days afterward. He hated that he couldn't lift the weights he did when he was younger. When the next week came around, Sam didn't want to go through the same cycle of pain and frustration again. He made an excuse and skipped the gym even though he felt guilty doing so.

Sam expected himself to perform at the same level he did when he was younger, but this only made exercising more difficult. As a result, he avoided the gym altogether. Underline any parts of this story that might apply to you. In later chapters, you will look at how to stop avoiding the things you fear by setting effective goals for change and putting these plans into action.

Bigger Life Problems

Both avoidant habits and self-criticism can cause you much bigger problems in your life. Avoiding any potential failure will keep you stuck in a rut of sameness. Working excessively hard to avoid making mistakes will leave you exhausted and demoralized. Criticizing yourself for *any* tiny mistake will leave you feeling defeated.

Each of the people we've discussed experience unfortunate consequences of their perfectionistic behaviors. Sometimes, it's the exact outcome they were hoping to avoid.

Jonas's rigid standards cause tension and distance in his family. He feels disappointed in his performance as a father and doesn't feel as close to his kids as he would like.

Natalie is so terrified of making a mistake and upsetting her manager that she becomes progressively slower in her work. Her manager becomes disappointed in her poor productivity rather than pleased with her accuracy.

Using her appearance and academic performance as the yardstick for her worth means Sofia's well-being is entirely dependent on how she performs in these areas, and it also alienates Sofia from her fellow students.

Setting too high standards for himself means that Sam misses opportunities for improving his fitness and health.

Before you move on, pause for a moment and look at the parts of these stories you've underlined so far. I wonder whether you have recognized some of your own battles in these examples. Which aspects of these stories reflect your life? Summarize your observations below.

_____

_____

_____

_____

_____

At first, it can be difficult to understand how perfectionism affects your life overall. After all, despite the many stereotypes applied to perfectionists, it looks different in everyone. You may only just be appreciating how many aspects of your life are affected by these unhelpful processes. In this next section, you'll explore your own unique patterns of perfectionism.

There's No Typical Perfectionist

In therapy, one of the reasons why unhelpful perfectionism may be overlooked is that it looks completely different from one person to the next. Many perfectionists have good jobs, get impressive results, win awards, and gain recognition. Yet inside they still feel like they are failing. Others become frozen, unable to start anything new because they are frightened that they will fail. My struggle with unhelpful perfectionism will look completely different from yours.

When I was in my early thirties, my husband and I bought a small business and grew it into a busy practice that provided executive coaching and leadership development around the country. I had a degree in psychology and had done further university study in coaching, where I got straight As for my assignments. While I understood the theory of coaching, I lacked confidence and experience. I wanted to be a good coach, but was scared that our executive clients would view me as incompetent. I would think back over my first clunky attempts at coaching and critique my performance as hopeless and incompetent.

Over several years, I subtly avoided coaching and instead gave the work to other coaches, preferring to stay behind the scenes. I didn't want to fail as a coach because it meant embarrassing myself in front of our employees, clients, and my husband. I made an important contribution to the success of the business and convinced myself that this was what I wanted.

Yet, because I could never accept the risk of failing, I never fully developed my coaching skills and instead watched as others did amazing work with clients. It was only years later, after I better understood my fear of failure, that I was able to stretch myself and finally develop these skills.

Each of the processes of perfectionism contributed to my struggle. The expectations I had of myself helped me achieve excellent grades in university, but made it difficult to master the practice of coaching because I wanted to never mess it up. I knew that if I made a mistake, I would criticize myself over and over. I feared failing so much I avoided doing coaching work altogether. As a result, I lost the opportunity to gain experience, develop my skills, and experience the satisfaction that comes from coaching. Now, let's have a look at how perfectionism looks in your life.

Checklist: Common Unhelpful Perfectionistic Behaviors

Unhelpful perfectionism drives a wide range of diverse behaviors. This activity will help you build a picture of your unhelpful perfectionism. Listed below are many common unhelpful perfectionistic behaviors. Check the ones that apply to you.

Work and Study

☐ Working excessively without enjoyment; feeling as if you *must* work this way to do things properly

☐ Repeatedly checking your work for mistakes

☐ Having difficulty being satisfied that your work is good enough or finished, creating multiple drafts, or having trouble handing work in

☐ Spending too long laboring over tasks that could be done quickly

☐ Procrastinating and experiencing difficulty completing tasks within deadlines

☐ Being excessively anxious about grades or work performance

☐ Getting caught up in the details and having difficulty seeing the broader context

☐ Having trouble making decisions, fearful of making the wrong choice

☐ Avoiding tasks or jobs that you aren't certain you can complete to a high standard

☐ Avoiding feedback and performance appraisals

☐ Avoiding or intensely fearing situations where you might be evaluated

☐ Passively avoiding opportunities that are challenging

☐ Persistently and excessively seeking reassurance about the quality of your work or performance

Home Life

☐ Needing things to be excessively neat

☐ Fearing other people will judge you harshly if things are out of place

☐ Needing to present a perfect home life to others

☐ Living in mess and clutter, or hoarding possessions

Family and Parenting

☐ Expecting perfect behavior from your children

☐ Having a low-tolerance for mistakes or mess

☐ Being irritable, losing your temper, or being critical of others

Relationships

☐ Feeling fearful of saying something wrong or stupid

☐ Always needing to say the right thing

☐ Worrying about being a good friend and not offending or hurting people

☐ Worrying about being judged negatively by others, or feeling anxious in social situations

☐ Withdrawing from social situations because you fear making a mistake or embarrassing yourself

☐ Seeking reassurance that people like you

☐ Being overly critical, fussy, or meticulous

☐ Other people finding you difficult to please

☐ Feeling constantly let down by others

☐ People around you feeling they aren't good enough for you

Appearance

☐ Needing to look or present perfectly

☐ Being overly critical or judgmental of your appearance

Health

☐ Being excessively focused on achieving perfect health behaviors such as a perfect diet or exercise routine

☐ Having difficulty starting or continuing with treatments or health routines

☐ Avoiding health activities because you can't do them properly

Hobbies, Sporting, and Creative Pursuits

☐ Having a limited range of interests beyond work/study

☐ Being reluctant to pursue interests because you can't do them to your standards

☐ Being anxious about your sporting, musical, or artistic performance

☐ Putting yourself under excessive pressure to perform

☐ Fearing failure and therefore not enjoying the activity

☐ Completely avoiding activities because you can't do them to your standards

Religion and Spirituality

☐ Needing to pray, worship, or adhere to rituals perfectly

☐ Being intolerant of your lapses of faith or practice or lapses by others

It can be uncomfortable to see these things written down on paper, so if you completed the checklist, well done. You may be realizing for the first time that quite a few of your daily habits could be related to unhelpful perfectionism and be wondering whether this will be a bigger challenge than you initially thought. Yet, only the habits that are causing you the most problems need to be the focus of your efforts to change. I'll explain why in Chapter 5. For now, briefly summarize what you've noticed so far about your unhelpful perfectionism by answering the following questions.

The biggest problem areas for me are:

1. _____

2. _____

3. _____

The items on the list that worry or upset me the most are:

1. _____

2. _____

3. _____

The habits I most want to change are:

1. _____

2. _____

3. _____

If you are feeling slightly concerned right now, that is completely understandable. Seeing this written down in black and white can be challenging. Unhelpful perfectionism may be affecting you more than you realize, and this might make you feel uneasy. After all, if you struggle with these issues, you can't be perfect. You may think, "I should be able to manage my perfectionism better!" You might feel an urge to put this book down and walk away. Would you be willing to stay with this process of discovery a bit longer if staying meant you could better manage your unhelpful perfectionism? I hope you'll stay.

Activity: Describe Your Own Experience of Unhelpful Perfectionism

Let's look at just one of the problem areas that you've checked in more detail. See if you can tease out the five processes of unhelpful perfectionism within the issue.

Briefly describe how your unhelpful perfectionistic behavior causes you problems.

_____

_____

_____

_____

_____

What excessive or inflexible standards do you set for yourself in this situation?

_____

_____

_____

_____

What kind of failure do you fear?

_____

_____

_____

_____

In what ways do you criticize yourself or your performance? What unkind, critical things might you say to yourself?

_____

_____

_____

_____

What things do you avoid so that you can avoid failing and the self-criticism that comes with this?

_____

_____

_____

_____

What are the negative consequences of this avoidance for you?

_____

_____

_____

_____

Take a moment to look back over what you've written. You may have found that this one unhelpful habit has many unwanted outcomes. Consider whether these outcomes extend across many other areas of your life. They may even affect your mood and well-being.

Could your perfectionism cause so many problems that it is linked to mental health problems that you might be experiencing? I feel a deep responsibility to make sure that as you work through this book you are safe and that I am giving you the support you need. So, please join me in this next section as we explore several common mental health problems and how they relate to unhelpful perfectionism.

Perfectionism and Mental Health Problems

While it can be extremely unhelpful, perfectionism is not considered a mental health disorder itself, even though some researchers have begun to use the term "clinical perfectionism" when it causes substantial distress and interferes with daily life. Many of the behaviors linked to unhelpful perfectionism overlap with other common mental health disorders, which may be another reason perfectionism can be missed in therapy. Let's explore the connection between perfectionism and mental health and how it might apply to you.

Rates of perfectionism and depression have been growing in Western societies over the past few decades (Curran and Hill 2019, Weinberger et al. 2018). In the United States, as many as 33.7 percent of people will experience anxiety in their lifetime (Bandelow and Michaelis 2015). Perfectionism is known to be a risk and maintaining factor for a large number of mental health disorders including depression, obsessive-compulsive disorder, social anxiety disorder, panic disorder, generalized anxiety disorder, post-traumatic stress disorder, eating disorders, body dysmorphic disorder, and chronic fatigue syndrome, professional burnout, hoarding disorder, and even suicide (Burgess et al. 2018, Egan, Wade, and Shafran 2012, Frost and Gross 1993, Timpano et al. 2011, Smith et al. 2018). We will focus on some of the more common closely related disorders in the coming pages.

Perfectionism, Eating Disorders, and Body-Image Problems

Many studies have shown perfectionism to be strongly linked to both eating disorders and negative body image. Eating and body image disturbances often develop when people strive to meet an ideal body shape through diet and exercise and have a specific goal for their weight or appearance. The warning signs of an eating disorder include:

- Constant worry about aspects of your appearance such as body shape, size, weight, and/or physical features

- Preoccupation with food and calories and feeling like this is taking over your life

- Periods when you restrict the amount that you eat to change your body shape or periods of eating excessively in a way that feels out of control

- Habits designed to ensure you don't gain weight such as dieting, vomiting, using laxatives, or excessive exercise

- Worries and unhelpful habits getting worse over time

Having difficulty with eating, weight, and body image is remarkably common. If these symptoms look familiar, I recommend you talk to your doctor. As these problems become more extreme, they can take over your life, cause serious medical complications, and can even be life-threatening, so please seek help if you struggle with this. With specialist help, you can relearn healthy eating habits, stabilize your weight, and refocus on other important aspects of your life. Working through this book is likely to help alongside this support.

Perfectionism and OCD

Sometimes, people who need things to be neat or like to be very organized describe themselves as "being a bit OCD;" however, this is misleading and understates the severe difficulties caused by this mental health disorder. OCD is a severe and debilitating disorder that makes normal life exceedingly difficult. It often gets worse over time and can take many years to be diagnosed and treated. The symptoms of OCD include:

- Persistent, worrying, and distressing thoughts or images that something terrible is going to happen, you will act on some unwanted urge, or you will make a tragic mistake that results in someone you love getting hurt or dying

- Feeling like you must do certain things to prevent this terrible outcome

- Intense uncomfortable sensations that you believe will not go away unless you do something to get rid of them

- Patterns of behavior designed to prevent, neutralize, or control the uncomfortable sensations, thoughts, images, and fear such as:

  - Avoiding things that trigger the worries

  - Repeatedly checking or counting

  - Repeating routine tasks

  - Needing things to be extremely exact or precise

  - Excessive cleaning or sanitizing

  - Reading or rewriting things; being unable to complete work unless it is exactly right

  - Lining up or organizing things into a certain order

  - Repeated mental rituals such as praying, reassuring yourself, or having a so-called positive thought

  - Seeking reassurance from others

- Having strong urges to continue doing these things to feel certain that the terrible outcome won't happen and discomfort won't come back

- Experiencing negative consequences in your life from these patterns of behavior because they take a lot of time or interfere with your life in other ways

If this seems familiar to you, I encourage you to seek out an experienced psychologist to help you explore what this means and, if needed, get you back on track. Some of this book is built upon some of the same strategies used to treat OCD, so many of the principles here will help. Alone, the book is unlikely to provide all the guidance you need.

Perfectionism and Anxiety

Perfectionism can feed your worries about the future by providing many examples of where things could go wrong. Many people with unhelpful perfectionism often feel anxious and worried in a way that is intense and overwhelming. If you worry about making mistakes in several different areas of your life and the worries feel uncontrollable and interfere with your day-to-day living, then you might have generalized anxiety disorder.

Other people have persistent worries about how they perform in social situations. When anxiety about social situations and relationships becomes persistent and debilitating, this is known as social anxiety disorder. You may have social anxiety disorder if you:

- Feel anxious and uneasy in most social situations

- Feel extremely nervous when meeting new people

- Constantly worry that you'll say something wrong, stupid, or awkward, or have difficulty talking at all

- Worry about people not liking you

- Constantly watch your behavior in social situations

- Have an intense fear of speaking in front of strangers

- Avoid social situations because you feel anxious

Due to the huge overlap between generalized anxiety, social anxiety, and perfectionism, the strategies in this book are likely to help, but I still recommend you seek professional guidance and support.

Perfectionism and Depression

Often treated as a medical condition, depression usually doesn't occur without a reason. Far more than a simple chemical imbalance, the causes of depression mostly come from the way people live their lives. You are more likely to experience depression if you become disconnected from meaningful work and other people, when you feel unsafe and insecure, or if you keep struggling with the painful parts of your personal history (Hari 2018). You will also feel sad and have low motivation when you are grieving, although it's important to distinguish between the normal process of grief and depression.

Unhelpful perfectionism makes living a fulfilling life more difficult. You may find it difficult to do the things you love because you fear making a mistake, or struggle to try something new because you might get it wrong. The influence of this on your mood can build slowly over time. Avoiding feeling uncomfortable leads to a life that is stressful and disappointing, and this in turn may intensify feelings of depression (Moroz and Dunkley 2018). If you also experience a constant stream of self-criticism, you might end up feeling exhausted and hopeless.

Nevertheless, it is important to recognize whether you have depression because it is an issue that can be addressed through psychological therapy. The symptoms of depression include:

- Feeling persistently sad, irritable, overwhelmed, miserable, guilty, or disappointed

- Lacking confidence

- Having feelings of worthlessness and hopelessness

- Experiencing low motivation and energy levels; feeling tired all the time

- Avoiding going out

- Withdrawing from friends and pleasurable activities

- Having difficulty concentrating

- Feeling life is not worth living

If you believe you might be depressed, please seek further professional help. If you are ever feeling extremely low, like your life is no longer worth living, please immediately seek help from friends, family, and professionals.

Let's take a moment to pause. It's challenging to consider how your daily struggles might be related to certain mental health problems. So, right now, look back over the questions that you completed at the end of the introduction, and complete the following sentences:

Two aspects of my perfectionism that I'd like to change are _____ and _____.

I would know my perfectionism was improving if I could _____.

_____, _____, and _____ are three positive changes I would see if my perfectionism were not such a problem anymore.

Now consider, if you achieved these things, how would your mood and mental health improve?

_____

_____

_____

_____

With such an interwoven relationship between perfectionism and mental health, it's not surprising that addressing your perfectionism is likely to help with other issues you are facing. Working through this book will help you reconnect with what is important and take real, tangible steps toward a life you love, even though you might feel worried, overwhelmed, or disheartened. Learning to be kinder to yourself by building your skills in self-compassion will also help to alleviate these feelings (Ferrari et al. 2018) and help you feel freer, more hopeful, and more able to enjoy things again. However, I will say just one more time: if you are experiencing serious mental health problems, you should also seek help from a licensed professional. It's important to get all the help that you need.

When Standards Become Unbreakable Rules

Have your expectations of yourself become strict rules, something that you must *always* achieve? Are they sometimes even impossible, such as striving for absolute perfection? Such standards tend to sound something like:

"I must always get an A"

"My home must always be clean and tidy"

"People must always like me"

"My children must always be well-behaved"

"I must always look my best"

Setting ambitious targets for yourself can be motivating and push you to achieve impressive results. However, if you expect to meet your standards for success *all the time* and keep raising these standards over time, it can cause many problems (Kobori, Hayakawa, and Tanno 2009). Rigid expectations will put you under enormous pressure. You will rarely meet your criterion for success, leaving you feeling frustrated and demoralized.

Activity: What Standards Do You Set for Yourself?

You may never have really questioned the yardstick that you use to measure success, so here is your opportunity. In the next activity, you will reflect on the rules you set for yourself and how tightly you hold them.

For each domain below, briefly describe the (often unspoken) expectations you have for yourself across different areas of your life. Then circle the number to rate whether you treat these standards as rigid rules or apply them more flexibly. I've included examples of both rigid rules and flexible objectives to guide you.

Relationships

Examples: "Everyone must like me all the time," "I must not offend anyone," or "I try to be a good friend."

Your Standards:

_____

_____

_____

I feel terrible if I don't meet this standard *all the time* (rigid rule).									I aim to achieve this, but feel okay in myself if I don't (flexible objective).
1	2	3	4	5	6	7	8	9	10

Parenting

Examples: "I must never get angry at my children," "I must never forget anything," or "I try to be organized."

Your Standards:

_____

_____

_____

I feel terrible if I don't meet   I aim to achieve this, but
this standard *all the time*   feel okay in myself if I don't
(rigid rule).   (flexible objective).

| 1 | 2 | 3 | 4 | 5 | 6 | 7 | 8 | 9 | 10 |

Work and Study

Examples: "I must perform exceptionally," or "I must never make a mistake."

Your Standards:

_____

_____

_____

I feel terrible if I don't meet   I aim to achieve this, but
this standard *all the time*   feel okay in myself if I don't
(rigid rule).   (flexible objective).

| 1 | 2 | 3 | 4 | 5 | 6 | 7 | 8 | 9 | 10 |

Health and Physical Appearance

Examples: "I must never eat junk food," "I must be thin," or "I try to look after my body."

Your Standards:

_____

_____

_____

I feel terrible if I don't meet this standard *all the time* (rigid rule).								I aim to achieve this, but feel okay in myself if I don't (flexible objective).	
1	2	3	4	5	6	7	8	9	10

Hobbies, Sports, or Creative Activities

Examples: "I must be the best at whatever I do," or "I like to finish things to a high standard."

Your Standards:

_____

_____

_____

I feel terrible if I don't meet this standard *all the time* (rigid rule).								I aim to achieve this, but feel okay in myself if I don't (flexible objective).	
1	2	3	4	5	6	7	8	9	10

Home Environment

Examples: "My house must always be clean and tidy," or "I like to keep things organized."

Your Standards:

_____

_____

_____

I feel terrible if I don't meet
this standard *all the time*
(rigid rule).

I aim to achieve this, but
feel okay in myself if I don't
(flexible objective).

1	2	3	4	5	6	7	8	9	10

Spiritual Practice

Examples: "I uphold the principles of my faith strictly at all times," or "I live by my faith's values."

Your Standards:

_____

_____

_____

I feel terrible if I don't meet
this standard *all the time*
(rigid rule).

I aim to achieve this, but
feel okay in myself if I don't
(flexible objective).

1	2	3	4	5	6	7	8	9	10

Helping Others

Examples: "I must prevent other people from suffering," or "I try to be helpful."

Your Standards:

_____

_____

_____

I feel terrible if I don't meet this standard *all the time* (rigid rule).								I aim to achieve this, but feel okay in myself if I don't (flexible objective).	
1	2	3	4	5	6	7	8	9	10

To complete this exercise, summarize your responses below.

In what areas of your life do you expect the most from yourself?

1. _____

2. _____

3. _____

In what areas of your life are your standards most inflexible?

1. _____

2. _____

3. _____

In what areas of your life are you more rigid about meeting your standards?

1. _____

2. _____

3. _____

You may have never considered how your inflexible personal standards could be causing you pressure and distress. Often how you feel about yourself will depend on whether you meet these standards. So, if these expectations keep getting higher, you are likely to feel bad about yourself *a lot of the time.*

Activity: How Do Your High Standards Make You Feel?

Take a moment to read the following script, then find a quiet, peaceful place to complete this activity. Some people find it difficult to visualize things, and if this applies to you, read the activity, write down your thoughts, then sit quietly for a few minutes and reflect on what you've written. An audio file of this activity can be found at http://www.newharbinger.com/48077.

Start by closing your eyes or looking down toward the floor, placing your feet squarely on the ground, and sitting up in your chair so that your back is straight and your head feels supported on your shoulders.

Begin by noticing the sensation of your body resting on the chair. Notice all the parts of your body that are touching the chair. Notice how your feet are resting on the floor. Let your body sink almost imperceptibly into the chair as if being gently pulled into the earth by gravity. Feel the support of the chair and the floor, holding you in place. Take a deep breath and cultivate a sense of calm.

Using the list above as a guide, choose one area of your life where it feels important to perform exceptionally well and where it is difficult to be satisfied with what you achieve. As if watching a movie, imagine a moment when you are striving to meet your expectations. Develop a rich picture of the scenario. Visualize where you are, the people you are with, and what you are saying. Notice what you are doing and watch how other people respond to you. Spend a couple of minutes developing this image.

Feel the pressure to achieve and the energy it takes to perform so well. Notice how the pressure to achieve feels inside your body. Notice physical sensations such as tension, tightness, heaviness, urgency, or agitation and where these occur in your body. Observe any urges to distract yourself—and yet, stay with the activity as best you can. Take a deep breath and observe these sensations for several minutes.

Now consider what would happen if you didn't meet your expectations. What if you are a terrible parent, fail at school, or get sacked from your job? Contemplate this possibility for a couple of minutes.

Identify any new feelings that bubble up as you think about this, such as embarrassment, fear, sadness, or shame. Notice any sensations of tension, tightness, heaviness, or agitation and where they occur in your body. Observe any urges to distract yourself—and yet, stay with the activity a little longer. Take a deep breath and observe these sensations for several minutes.

Now take one long, deep breath and slowly bring this activity to an end. Allow a feeling of calm to flow through your body. Breathe deeply and slowly. Feel your feet resting on the floor and your body resting on the chair. When you are ready, open your eyes and return to the day.

If you found this activity difficult, I am still glad that you gave it a go. There will be several more opportunities to sit quietly and reflect on your experiences throughout this book, and I encourage you to try out these activities as best you can, in whatever manner is possible for you. Now take this opportunity to reflect on your experience by answering the following questions.

Briefly describe the situation that you imagined during the activity:

_____

_____

_____

_____

Briefly describe what you expected of yourself in that situation (your personal standard):

_____

_____

_____

_____

What emotions came up when you were striving to meet your expectations? Circle any of the examples listed below that applied to you, adding anything else you noticed underneath.

motivated	inspired	excited
anxious	overwhelmed	fearful
pressured	guilty	stressed

_____   _____   _____

_____   _____   _____

What emotions came up when you imagined *not* meeting your expectations? Circle any of the examples listed below that applied to you, adding any others underneath.

fearful	overwhelmed	disappointed
ashamed	guilty	embarrassed
sad	worthless	helpless

_____   _____   _____

_____   _____   _____

What body sensations did you notice during this visualization activity? Circle any of the following you experienced, adding any others underneath:

tension	restlessness	energized
heaviness	churning	tightness
agitation	shakiness	emptiness

_____   _____   _____

_____   _____   _____

There is nothing wrong with aiming for greatness and working hard toward success. The problems come when your aspirations become rules that you must achieve all the time. As you work through this book, you will explore different ways to approach your expectations. While you do not need to lower your standards, you may benefit from being more flexible in how you approach them. My goal is to help you to strive for the results that you want in a healthy, flexible way that works better for you.

Putting It Together

While helpful perfectionism is associated with flourishing, unhelpful perfectionism can interfere with every aspect of your life, causing you to flounder rather than flourish and sometimes even struggle to achieve your goals at all. Unhelpful perfectionism can also cause conflict in your relationships and is linked to many common mental health problems.

There are five processes that are typical of unhelpful perfectionism. Setting standards for yourself that are excessively ambitious and inflexible and having an intense fear of failure both lead to criticizing yourself when you don't meet your ideals and avoiding many different situations to reduce your fear. These responses can then cause much bigger issues in your life.

The goal of this book is to help you transform the unhelpful aspects of your perfectionism into something that works for you without needing to lower your standards. Where your standards have become rigid rules, you'll learn to respond more flexibly and do what is important, despite your fear of failing, by applying the techniques from Acceptance and Commitment Therapy. Developing skills in self-compassion from Compassion-Focused Therapy will help you to be kinder to yourself as you work toward your goals. These skills have opened my life in many exciting ways, and I believe that you will find this too. Thank you for entrusting me with helping you. I can't wait for us to work on this together.

Taking Small, Imperfect Steps: Your Personal Action Plan

At the end of each chapter, you'll find space to reflect on what you've discovered and write down the steps that you are going to take as a result. So, before you move on, take the time to develop your first Personal Action Plan.

What did you learn in this chapter that was relevant to you?

1. _____

2. _____

3. _____

What did you learn about yourself?

1. _____

2. _____

3. _____

Over the coming days, what small actions would you be willing to take toward a life where your perfectionism is more helpful for you?

1. _____

2. _____

3. _____

CHAPTER 2

Seeking Perfection to Escape the Shame of Failure

Our doubts are traitors, and make us lose the good we oft might win, by fearing to attempt.

—William Shakespeare, from *Measure for Measure*

Fear of failure is a common and well-documented problem, and a simple Google search will result in thousands of pages of advice such as "Ten Signs You Might Have a Fear of Failure," "How to Overcome Your Fear of Failure," and "How to Stop Living in Fear." These articles present fear of failure as a problem to be solved and something that can be fixed through simple steps. Often, the suggestion is that you must rid yourself of fear because it stops you from pursuing your goals.

Popular culture also idolizes stories of failures that are turned into success. Richard Branson, founder of the Virgin Group, is known to have dropped out of high school. Vera Wang was not selected for the 1968 US Olympic figure skating team, which prompted her to take a job at *Vogue* and pursue a career in fashion. Abraham Lincoln failed in business in 1831 and his first run for president in 1856, before being elected sixteenth president in 1861. Dr. Seuss's first book, *And to Think I Saw It on Mulberry Street,* was rejected twenty-eight times before being accepted for publication. JK Rowling, who is possibly the most cited, recent example of "failure-turned-success" was a divorced, depressed, single parent before writing the famous *Harry Potter* books.

Yet, despite well-intentioned advice that "mistakes are an opportunity to do better the next time" and being offered "twenty inspirational quotes that will help you overcome fear of failure," many of us continue to struggle with the fear that we will make a mistake, be unsuccessful, or get rejected. In this chapter, you will have an opportunity to look more deeply at *your* fear of failure and how it drives many of your unhelpful perfectionistic habits.

What Is Fear of Failure?

Fear of failure is the fear that you will make a mistake or cause something to go wrong, leaving you feeling guilty, embarrassed, ashamed, and humiliated. A "failure" can be any outcome where you do not meet your own expectations. Failures can include:

- Making a mistake in your work or assignment such as spelling, grammar, or calculations

- Getting feedback on your performance

- Forgetting something such as locking your keys in the car or missing an appointment

- Looking silly or embarrassing yourself such as by tripping or getting lost

- Saying the wrong thing or being awkward

- Not being liked or not being invited

- Hurting someone's feelings

- Being rejected by others

- Not meeting the expectations of others

- Not achieving any goal you've set for yourself

If you fear failure, you'll find these experiences intensely uncomfortable and have a powerful urge to avoid them.

Activity: Exploring Your Fear of Failure

Below, you will find listed many types of "failure" that make people feel uncomfortable. The more uncomfortable something makes you feel, the more you are likely to fear it and try to avoid it. In this activity, you will estimate how uncomfortable each experience would be for you. Mark your answer on the line with an X.

Situation	Intensity of Discomfort									
1. Making a mistake in your work	Not at all intense									Extremely intense
	1	2	3	4	5	6	7	8	9	10

Situation	Intensity of Discomfort									
2. Getting feedback on your performance	Not at all intense									Extremely intense
	1	2	3	4	5	6	7	8	9	10
3. Forgetting something	Not at all intense									Extremely intense
	1	2	3	4	5	6	7	8	9	10
4. Looking silly and embarrassing yourself	Not at all intense									Extremely intense
	1	2	3	4	5	6	7	8	9	10
5. Saying the wrong thing	Not at all intense									Extremely intense
	1	2	3	4	5	6	7	8	9	10
6. Not being liked	Not at all intense									Extremely intense
	1	2	3	4	5	6	7	8	9	10
7. Hurting someone's feelings	Not at all intense									Extremely intense
	1	2	3	4	5	6	7	8	9	10
8. Being rejected by others	Not at all intense									Extremely intense
	1	2	3	4	5	6	7	8	9	10
9. Not meeting the expectations of others	Not at all intense									Extremely intense
	1	2	3	4	5	6	7	8	9	10
10. Not achieving a goal you've set	Not at all intense									Extremely intense
	1	2	3	4	5	6	7	8	9	10

List the three areas that make you feel most uncomfortable (discomfort is the most intense).

1. _____

2. _____

3. _____

When could your response to these situations be out of proportion to the actual risk?

_____

_____

_____

Sometimes, fear of failure is more intense than you might expect from the size or implications of the actual mistake. Nothing listed above would cause you injury or death, although they might cause embarrassment, inconvenience, or sadness. The intensity of your response, however, might be closer to something that would do you serious, permanent harm. So, it is no wonder that you would work hard to avoid these things happening. Unhelpful habits develop as a way of managing this intense fear of failure. Yet, while avoiding the things that make you feel uncomfortable makes perfect sense in the short term, it can cause much bigger problems in the long term. This is why fear of failure forms a central part of unhelpful perfectionism.

Fear of Failure Sits at the Heart of Unhelpful Perfectionism

In this section, you will explore how fear of failure is the key driver of unhelpful perfectionistic behaviors as you map out the five processes of unhelpful perfectionism. At first, you'll explore two people who struggle with fear of failure: Mei Ling and John. Then, you'll have an opportunity to map your own unhelpful perfectionistic patterns.

Mei Ling was a high-performing student with an excellent GPA. She worked extremely hard on every assignment to make sure she kept up her average, spending days on each assignment and often staying up late at night. Yet, at the end of her second year, Mei Ling made a mistake on her final report, leaving out an entire section and handing it in incomplete. The next day, Mei Ling suddenly realized her mistake when talking to her friends. Immediately flooded with feelings of embarrassment and shame, Mei Ling's face went red and she felt hot all over. Within moments, she felt sick to her stomach, dizzy, and thought she might vomit. Quickly, Mei Ling made an excuse to leave, and once on her own, began to cry. For the rest of the week, Mei Ling avoided her friends. Alone in her room, she went over and over her mistake, angry at herself and calling herself "hopeless" and "a loser." The only thing that made her feel better was deciding that she would work much harder next year to make up for this mistake and that from then on, she would double-check all her work before handing it in.

Here is how each of the five processes of unhelpful perfectionism are interwoven in Mei Ling's story.

Process 1: Excessively High and Inflexible Standards	
The excessive and inflexible standards Mei Ling sets for herself are:	"I must maintain an excellent GPA at all times."
Process 2: Fear of Failure	
The failure Mei Ling fears most is:	"Getting a bad grade and my friends seeing me as a failure."
The uncomfortable emotions and physical sensations associated with that fear are:	Feeling embarrassed, ashamed, and scared. Face going red, feeling hot all over, sick to her stomach, dizzy, feeling like she might vomit, and crying.
Process 3: Relentless Self-Criticism	
Mei Ling criticizes herself by saying:	"I am hopeless." "I am a loser."
Process 4: Unhelpful Avoidance	
Unhelpful avoidance strategies used by Mei Ling are:	Spending even more time working on her assignments and thoroughly checking them.
Process 5: Bigger Life Problems	
The bigger life problems caused by Mei Ling's avoidance are likely to be:	Working even harder could lead to exhaustion and burnout. Withdrawing from her friends could lead to being socially isolated.

Mei Ling had an extreme response to her mistake. While the consequence of her mistake would have been negligible on her overall grade, this is irrelevant for Mei Ling; she had failed to meet her standards and felt extremely disappointed in herself. Mei Ling's response follows a common perfectionistic pattern of rigid expectations, extreme distress, and avoiding future failures by working even harder.

Failure often feels even worse when other people see it. Mistakes that cause social embarrassment can feel unbearable. Humans are social animals. A small mistake made on your own may be judged a complete failure when others see it, triggering feelings of shame and embarrassment. Let's explore how this plays out for John.

A few months after John started an exciting new job, he organized a night out with his work team. Believing it's important that everyone see him as a cool and friendly guy, John picked a trendy new bar as the venue and sent an email with the details. John thought this bar would have a hip vibe but on the night of the event, the group arrived to find the bar empty and dull. John was horrified. He was sure everyone would think he was boring and uncool. His heart began to race and he broke out in a sweat. While everyone else had an enjoyable time, John remained restless and uneasy all night. He tried to smile and chat, but inside, he was going over and over his mistake. Unable to relax and enjoy himself, John headed home early. Over the weekend, when John thought about the moment he and his colleagues arrived and found the bar empty, he felt drained and dejected. He was certain that everyone would think he was a loser. On Monday, John was too embarrassed to mention the night out and kept to himself all day. John didn't organize any more nights out, believing that no one would want to go out with him anyway.

Now, it is your turn to tease out John's unhelpful perfectionistic processes using the story above as a guide.

Process 1: Excessively High and Inflexible Standards	
The excessive and inflexible standards John sets for himself are:	
Process 2: Fear of Failure	
The failure John fears most is:	
The uncomfortable emotions and physical sensations associated with that fear are:	

Process 3: Relentless Self-Criticism	
John criticizes himself by saying:	
Process 4: Unhelpful Avoidance	
Unhelpful avoidance strategies used by John are:	
Process 5: Bigger Life Problems	
The bigger life problems caused by John's avoidance are likely to be:	

For Mei Ling and John, the emotional reaction they experience after making a mistake is immediate and overwhelming. Each of them then changes their behavior to avoid this happening again, potentially causing bigger problems down the road. Now it's your turn to explore the habits you've developed to manage your fear of failure.

Activity: Unpacking Your Own Unhelpful Perfectionism

In this activity, you'll explore how your fear of failure drives your unhelpful perfectionistic habits. I realize this might not be easy. You may rarely make mistakes or feel reluctant to write something down that is so embarrassing. I know it can be excruciating to think about mistakes you've made; however, I can assure you that there is value in thinking about this. By learning about what you fear and how you respond, you can begin to respond differently.

So, using your answers to the first questionnaire and the examples above as inspiration, describe a failure, mistake, or social error you've committed that made you feel particularly uncomfortable. Let me reassure you: writing it down will not make the situation or outcome any worse!

_____

_____

_____

_____

_____

Now complete the table below, breaking this experience down into the five processes of unhelpful perfectionism.

Process 1: Excessively High and Inflexible Standards	
The excessive and inflexible standards I set for myself are:	
Process 2: Fear of Failure	
The failure I fear most is:	
The uncomfortable emotions and physical sensations associated with that fear are:	
Process 3: Relentless Self-Criticism	
I criticize myself by saying:	
Process 4: Unhelpful Avoidance	
Unhelpful avoidance strategies I use are:	
Process 5: Bigger Life Problems	
The bigger life problems caused by my avoidance are likely to be:	

How did you feel as you wrote this down? Often, just remembering a mistake can bring back the same uncomfortable feelings you felt at the time, so if you completed this, I congratulate you on choosing to face your discomfort. I hope by completing this you are beginning to see the role fear of failure plays in your unhelpful perfectionism. Now let's delve even deeper into these fears by exploring your "Big Bad."

Getting to Know Your "Big Bad"

The term "Big Bad" originated on the show *Buffy the Vampire Slayer.* The Big Bad was the villain or nemesis whom the hero fought throughout the season. This term now extends to other series. In *Harry Potter*, the Big Bad is Lord Voldemort; in *Doctor Who*, it is The Master; in Marvel movies, it is Thanos; and in *Batman*, it is The Joker. In perfectionism, the Big Bad is the fear of failure that you keep fighting.

Each of the people we've discussed so far also has their own Big Bad. If you asked Mei Ling, she might say:

"I must never make a mistake because if I do, I might get a bad grade. If I get a bad grade, it means that I am stupid."

John's Big Bad might be something like:

"People must always think I am a cool, hip person. If they don't, they'll think I am boring and they won't like me."

Personally, my Big Bad is that I am incompetent in some way. It's a fear that relates to most of my unhelpful perfectionistic behaviors and keeps coming up in my life. I can think of many examples of this fear in my life.

When my kids were small, I would feel mortified if they were rude in public such as scowling instead of saying thank you, having more than their share of cake at a party, or having a meltdown in the supermarket. I was certain my kids' behavior reflected my parenting and I felt ashamed. I was afraid I was not a good parent (incompetent, my Big Bad). Whenever something went wrong, I would feel rising tension and my head would feel as if it was going to explode. I could quickly become overwhelmed by these sensations and respond by focusing more on my kids' behavior. I'd lecture my children on their manners and implement reward charts and consequences to try to get things on track. Eventually, I learned to recognize that my need to be a perfect mom and fear of failing was driving my behavior. I learned to slow down, take a few deep breaths, and not react until I was calmer. While I'm not perfect at this, I have become better at recognizing those times and choosing to be more consistent and patient as a mother.

Here's another example of my Big Bad in a different context:

As a therapist, I sometimes worry that my clients won't improve. I start to think that if they don't get better, it's because I am not good enough as a therapist. I can have persistent thoughts like

"They should see a therapist who is more skilled than me," or "I don't know how to help this client." I feel scared that I am incompetent as a therapist and respond by working harder, studying more, attending more training, and always trying to do better. Mostly, this works out okay, but when I'm in a difficult session, these doubts can cause problems. I can get caught up in my worries, distracted by my unhelpful thoughts, and my attention can be pulled away from the client. I can feel tense, uneasy, and have a churning feeling in my stomach. Over time and with practice, I've learned to recognize this fear. With effort, I can choose to slow down, listen, and return to being useful however I can.

Now it's your turn to reflect on the deeper fear that underpins your perfectionism and that you try to avoid. You'll start this process in a quiet, reflective space by doing a visualization exercise. Afterward, you will better appreciate the deeper fears that lie beneath your unhelpful behaviors.

Activity: Your Big Bad

Take a moment to read the following script, then find a quiet, peaceful place to complete this activity. As before, if you find it difficult to visualize things, read the script, write down your thoughts, then sit quietly to reflect on what you've written. You'll have a similar benefit. An audio file of this activity can be found at http://www.newharbinger.com/48077.

Start by closing your eyes or looking down toward the floor, placing your feet squarely on the ground and sitting up in your chair so that your back is straight and your head feels supported on your shoulders.

Begin by noticing the sensation of your body resting on the chair. Notice all the parts of your body that are touching the chair. Notice how your feet are resting on the floor. Let your body be pulled gently into the earth by gravity and feel the support of the chair holding you in place. Take a few deep breaths and cultivate a sense of calm.

Think about a mistake you've made in the past. As if you were watching yourself in a movie while the sound was turned down, imagine yourself making this mistake. (I know this is uncomfortable.)

Notice where you are, the people you are with, and what you are saying. Observe what you are doing, and if there are other people involved, watch how they respond to you in that moment. Consider the following questions:

1. What is the worst thing that could happen if this mistake were to occur?

2. What does this mistake say about you?

Allow some time for your mind to contemplate these questions. Allow your thoughts to drift by for several minutes.

Notice how you feel. Find and label at least one emotion that you are experiencing right now such as sadness, worry, doubt, guilt, shame, or embarrassment. Try to explore these emotions without fighting them.

Notice any physical sensations such as tension, tightness, heaviness, or agitation and where they are in your body. If this feels too intense, see if you can stay with these sensations for just a moment before taking a deep, calming breath.

With several slow breaths, gently bring this activity to an end. Allow a feeling of calm to flow throughout your body with each breath. Feel your feet resting on the floor and your body resting on the chair. When you are ready, open your eyes and return to the room, letting go of your discomfort and taking this feeling of calm with you.

Briefly describe the situation you imagined.

_____

_____

_____

_____

_____

What aspects of this situation were most uncomfortable for you?

_____

_____

_____

_____

What could this mistake say about you as a person?

_____

_____

_____

_____

It can be difficult to recognize your own Big Bad. So, below, I've listed some examples of the Big Bads that my clients have identified while in therapy. Place a checkmark against any Big Bads that feel familiar to you and underline the one that seems most frightening.

☐   Other people negatively judging you

☐   Being incompetent

☐   Being seen by others as incompetent

☐   Not being liked, respected, or admired

☐   Not being good enough

☐   Not being enough

☐   Not being smart enough

☐   Being a failure as a person

☐   Being a failure in your work

☐   Failing in relationships

☐   Experiencing destitution or becoming penniless or homeless

Phew…that is an intense list. Take a moment to reflect on what *your* Big Bad might be and note it down here:

_____

_____

_____

_____

_____

If you completed these activities, you've done some of the most challenging work in this book. It takes courage to explore areas of yourself that are dark and uncomfortable, especially when it makes you feel embarrassed or ashamed.

Running from Feelings of Shame

Mistakes and failure can trigger feelings of shame. Shame emerges when you make a mistake or something bad happens—and you believe it is your fault because there is something wrong with you (Gilbert 2017, Gilbert, McEwan, et al. 2010). Shame is an acutely painful experience that combines strong emotions with these negative self-judgments and evaluations. When you feel shame, you see yourself as defective, broken, or inadequate. You may want to hide from others because you feel worthless, embarrassed, or disgusted and assume others will judge you the same way too.

When Saanvi compared herself to the professional models in the media, she felt ugly and inadequate. Even though she knew the images were digitally enhanced, she still idealized these women as the peak of beauty. However, Saanvi's body shape would never match this ideal. Shorter, with a curvy frame and an oval face, Saanvi lacked the angular form she believed was attractive. She felt a deep hatred of her body and thought of herself as a failure for not working out hard enough and for eating foods she shouldn't. Saanvi avoided wearing form-fitting clothes and instead hid her body, feeling shame and sadness that it would never look the way she wanted.

All emotions have corresponding physical sensations in the body, and shame is no different. Feeling nervous can lead to butterflies in the stomach and losing a relationship can result in heartache. Shame feels so uncomfortable, most people will go to great lengths to avoid feeling this way.

Close your eyes for a moment and scan your body, remembering how it feels when you make a mistake. Then, place a checkmark against anything in the following list that seems familiar to you.

Physical Location	Common Sensations			
In your chest:	☐	Tension	☐	Heaviness
	☐	Tightness	☐	Restlessness
In your stomach:	☐	Churning/twisting	☐	Tightness
	☐	Nausea/feeling sick	☐	Heaviness
	☐	Lurching	☐	Falling/sinking/dropping
Elsewhere in your body:	☐	Muscle tension	☐	Mind spinning
	☐	Agitation	☐	Foggy mind
	☐	Restlessness	☐	Shakiness
	☐	Headache	☐	Hands fidgeting

I know exactly what the shame of making a mistake feels like for me: it's a lurching feeling in my stomach and a restless, unsettled feeling throughout my entire body. Take a moment to describe what this feels like for you:

When I make a mistake, I feel _____, _____, and _____ in my body.

The shame you experience when making a mistake is why mistakes are so painful, and why you try so hard to avoid them. Learning to recognize these feelings as they happen will allow you to notice how you respond, whether helpful or unhelpful. This early warning can also give you a chance to do something different.

Activity: Noticing Your Discomfort

In this activity, you will pay attention to the inner sensations that you experience with mistakes and failure. At the top of the page, note down the sensations you are tracking (the sensations associated with mistakes and failure) and the Big Bad that underlies your fear of failure.

Then, whenever you feel the sensations, note down what you are doing in that moment (the situation), what you are fearful might happen (the potential or actual mistake), *and* how you respond (what you do as a result). Pay close attention to any time you try to get rid of the sensations such as by leaving the situation or putting something off until later.

Throughout the week, log your observations using the sheet below. The first two logs are some examples; the third one is blank for your own use. A printable version of this sheet can also be found at http://www.newharbinger.com/48077.

Observation Sheet: Noticing Your Discomfort (Example 1)

Physical sensations I am tracking: Stomach—churning and twisting

My Big Bad: People won't like me

Situation	What I worry will happen (feared mistake)	What I do to manage these feelings
Getting ready for a night out with friends	I'll be awkward, say something stupid, and people won't like me.	Repeatedly check my appearance in the mirror. Worry about what I will talk about.
Making a presentation to my team	I'll be too boring and people will think I'm a dull person.	Practice my presentation over and over. Spend hours thinking up light-hearted jokes and finding suitable images.
Choosing a restaurant for dinner with my friends	I can't decide. What if they don't like what I choose and are angry at me or disappointed?	I check with my friends over and over until I am sure that everyone is happy.

Observation Sheet: Noticing Your Discomfort (Example 2)

Physical sensations I am tracking: Tension in my chest and a sinking feeling in my stomach

My Big Bad: I am incompetent

Situation	What I worry will happen (feared mistake)	What I do to manage these feelings
Sending an email to a client	I'll make a mistake in what I've written. People will think I'm useless.	Check the email several times and reassure myself it was okay.
Starting a new exercise program	I'll start this exercise program, spend a lot of money, then just stop soon afterward. I'll just end up giving up and never getting fit.	Reluctantly attend the exercise program, but feel uncomfortable the whole time.
Finishing and sending a report	The report won't be good enough and I'll get a bad grade.	Keep working on the report late into the night, checking and rechecking my work.

Observation Sheet: Noticing Your Discomfort

Physical sensations I am tracking: _____

My Big Bad: _____

Situation	What I worry will happen (feared mistake)	What I do to manage these feelings

Before you move on, look back to find any common patterns within your responses. Over the coming week, keep looking for the same sensations and continue to log them on the tracking sheet. This will further develop your ability to notice (and accommodate) the uncomfortable inner experiences that come with fear of failure.

Well done for completing this activity. Once again, you've chosen to tune into something that is uncomfortable and that you would prefer to avoid. This takes courage and commitment. If you haven't done this activity quite yet, there's still time. This task is another important foundation for positive change, so I encourage you to give it a go. It is amazing what you can learn when you pay full attention to what your body is telling you and how you respond.

Asking you to pay attention to things that are uncomfortable is a deliberate choice on my part. By completing this task, you are developing your awareness and ability to stay with uncomfortable emotions and sensations. The more you learn to acknowledge how you feel, slow down, make room, and label these experiences, the more ability you will have to respond in new, helpful ways. This will help you begin to transform your unhelpful habits into helpful behaviors that support your learning, ability to take risks, and personal growth.

Fear Is Not a Problem You Need to Solve

Even though the thoughts, emotions, and sensations that you've been describing may be vivid and powerful, fear itself not something that you need to change. I appreciate that, at first, I might seem crazy saying this. After all, it is understandable to avoid feeling afraid. Most people would prefer to feel safe and comfortable—except when they choose to go sky diving, ride a rollercoaster, or watch a scary movie. So, hey, I guess many of us don't want to avoid this all the time.

If you have been avoiding mistakes so that you feel less worried and uncomfortable, how is this working out for you? Over the years of avoiding failure, have you ended up feeling less fearful, more fearful, or do you have the same amount of fear of failing? (Circle one answer below.)

Over time my fear of failure has: Lessened   Stayed the same   Increased

Fear is an involuntary, unlearned, and biological response that evolved to prepare you to take appropriate action when you are in danger. It is a normal human emotion, and as such, not something you can or need to change. For our ancestors living in the savannah, desert, or jungle, daily threats included predators, starvation, weather, illness, and isolation. Any significant mistake could have threatened your survival such as not finding enough food to eat, being attacked by a predator, or being rejected from your tribe. In modern times, your fears can get distorted and out of touch with reality. The threats you face today are quite different from those your ancestors had on the savannah—most of us in Western society are unlikely to die of starvation or be eaten by a predator.

If you are someone who strives to achieve exceptional or flawless results, mistakes and potential failure have become an imagined threat to your well-being, livelihood, and social standing. Striving for perfection involves actively looking for errors of any kind whether past, current, real, imagined, or predicted. By continually searching for mistakes and contemplating failure, you will reignite your fear response and perpetuate unhelpful cycles of anxiety and avoidance.

Yet, even though fear seems like something you should avoid, it is not the problem that needs to be solved. You can learn, instead, to respond in different ways. The first step is to learn how to center yourself when you feel overwhelmed by fear. You'll do this using Soothing Rhythm Breathing. This technique is so useful that I'm introducing it early in the book to give you plenty of opportunities to practice.

Soothing Rhythm Breathing is a technique from CFT that will help you to calm and anchor yourself when you are distressed or overwhelmed (Kolts 2016, Welford 2016, Silberstein-Tirch 2019).

One important thing to note here: Soothing Rhythm Breathing is *not* a way to get rid of your uncomfortable emotions. Instead, it is a way of stabilizing yourself in the midst of your struggle so that you can make better decisions and step toward the things that you fear. As you learn this skill, use the sense of calm you generate to find greater clarity and courage to face your fears rather than escape them.

I recommend practicing Soothing Rhythm Breathing daily if possible, starting with just a few minutes at a time. Brief, regular practice can help you activate your parasympathetic nervous system and find greater calm in your life.

Activity: Soothing Rhythm Breathing

Read the following script, then find a quiet, peaceful place to complete this practice. Alternatively, an audio file of this activity can be found at http://www.newharbinger.com/48077.

Start by closing your eyes or looking down toward the floor, placing your feet squarely on the ground and sitting up in your chair so that your back is straight and your head feels supported on your shoulders.

Begin by noticing the feeling of your body resting on the chair. Notice all the parts of your body that are touching the chair. Notice how your feet are resting on the floor. Open your chest by gently rolling your shoulders back and feel the space for your lungs expand.

Focus on your breath. Notice the many different sensations of breathing; the gentle rise and fall of your chest, the gentle push of your lungs into your stomach, and the feeling of your lungs expanding and contracting. Continue this way for several minutes.

Now gradually slow down your breath. Take longer and longer with your in-breath, pausing for two to three seconds before you slowly breathe out. Don't force it. Allow your muscles to relax and expand. It may help to count in your mind, gradually deepening and lengthening your breath as follows:

"IN – 2 – 3 – HOLD – OUT – 2 – 3"

Remember to deeply open your lungs, feeling them expand deep into your stomach. Should your mind get caught up with thinking at any time, gently bring your attention back to the rise and fall of your chest and the sensation of slowing down. Gradually, lengthen each breath in and out to four to five seconds, silently counting:

"IN – 2 – 3 – 4 – HOLD – 2 – 3 – OUT – 2 – 3 – 4"

Allow yourself to settle into a speed that feels comfortable and natural to you. Continue this way for several minutes. Let your face soften, jaws and shoulders relax, and a gentle smile form on your face. Notice what it feels like in your body to breathe in this relaxed, slow, and soothing way. Continue this way for several more minutes.

After several minutes of breathing this way, gently bring the activity to a close. Acknowledge your effort in taking the time to practice in this way. Open your eyes, look around, move, or stretch your body gently, and return to your day.

Take a moment to note down your responses to the following questions.

What sensations did you notice in your body during and after this practice?

_____

_____

_____

When could you practice this skill across the coming week and beyond?

_____

_____

_____

Putting It Together

Unhelpful perfectionism is behavior designed to move you away from something you fear. At the center of perfectionism is always some kind of fear of failure. It can feel devastating, triggering uncomfortable thoughts like "I am a loser" or "I am hopeless" and physical sensations such as feeling tense, agitated, or even sick to the stomach.

Beneath your fear lies your Big Bad. As the thing you most want to avoid, most of your perfectionistic worries will lead back to your Big Bad. Making a mistake might remind you that you are never good enough. Someone not returning your text might remind you that you are unlikable. Your Big Bad often comes with profound feelings of shame and sadness.

All these experiences are so unpleasant, of course, you want to avoid them. They may be so uncomfortable that you may even feel afraid of them. So, you focus hard on not making mistakes and making sure people like you—doing whatever it takes. To avoid any mistakes, you might have paid close attention to potential risks and prepared for worst-case scenarios.

However, what if your fear serves an important function and is not a problem to be solved? By avoiding risks, you'll miss many enjoyable things and end up drifting away from a life you love. Throughout the remainder of this book, you will explore how to feel the fear and all the uncomfortable sensations that come with it—and still move toward the things that are important to you.

Taking Small, Imperfect Steps: Your Personal Action Plan

Take a minute to create your Personal Action Plan for this chapter.

What did you learn in this chapter that was relevant to you?

1. _____

2. _____

3. _____

What did you learn about yourself?

1. _____

2. _____

3. _____

Over the coming days, what small actions would you be willing to take toward a life where your perfectionism is more helpful for you?

1. _____

2. _____

3. _____

Is Perfectionism Controlling Your Life?

Tilly was downcast; as with all perfectionists, it was the detail others might not notice that destroyed for her the pleasure of achievement.

—Elspeth Huxley, *The Flame Trees of Thika*

Think back to your earliest memory of wanting to be perfect. Perhaps, you threw away a drawing because the lines weren't neat enough or stopped playing a sport because you couldn't do it well. Maybe you fretted about your grades late into the night as you pursued a perfect score. Or maybe when your friends laughed at you falling over in the playground, you ran and hid, too ashamed to be seen.

Over time, these small actions may have become long-term habits. No longer just throwing out your artwork because it isn't good enough, you might have dropped out of art, drama, and music because you couldn't do them well. Maybe you now work hard to please your boss, your clients, or your family, forgetting your own needs. Perhaps you stay home and avoid your friends because you said something awkward or stupid. These long-term habits can make life difficult.

This chapter is about finding out what your unhelpful perfectionism is costing you: the opportunities you've missed and the emotional burden you've carried by never meeting your standards. We'll explore how you developed these habits and why you keep repeating them even when they cause you problems. By the end of this chapter, you'll have a much clearer idea of what you can change to move you toward a more fulfilling life.

What Does Your Perfectionism Really Cost?

Perfectionism presents you with a challenge: trying to achieve your ambitious standards while avoiding any chance of failure. There are several different ways people respond to this challenge. Some work harder, pushing themselves to achieve more and checking everything they do to avoid mistakes.

Others give up when they realize they can't meet their perfectionistic ideals, feeling crushed by their self-criticism and their fear of failing. How about you? Circle a number on the line below that reflects your approach to this challenge.

I work harder and harder to be perfect.								I feel disheartened, hopeless, and tend to give up.	
1	2	3	4	5	6	7	8	9	10

If your answer is at either end, you have a distinctive way of approaching the challenge of perfectionism. Or, maybe your answer depends on the situation; you withdraw from some situations and push yourself hard in others. Either way, somehow you must find an approach that is flexible, effective, and does not leave you worn out, exhausted, isolated, or defeated.

Working Harder Leads to Stress and Burnout

Like a wolf in sheep's clothing, perfectionism offers a false promise that you can gain control of your life by working harder, preventing mistakes, attaining more things, or accomplishing difficult tasks. Could you have fallen for this illusion? Check any of the following statements that apply to you.

☐ I feel like I must make the most out of every minute of my day

☐ I must always be working toward something

☐ I find it hard to do nothing

☐ I never feel at ease

☐ I get frustrated, irritable, or angry when things don't work out well

☐ I always push myself to do my best

☐ I must always please everyone

☐ I always feel under pressure

Living on a hamster wheel of busy-ness can cost you a sense of peace, calm, and satisfaction replaced with pressure, irritability, and stress. How stressed are you? Circle the answer that best fits your experience.

I generally feel relaxed	I have an average amount of stress	I sometimes feel quite wound up	I often get really stressed-out and overwhelmed	I feel under enormous pressure all the time

Perfectionism is related to chronic stress and physical health problems (Smith et al. 2017). The symptoms of stress include low energy, difficulty sleeping, aches, pains, tense muscles, stomach or digestion problems, headaches, frequent colds or infections, irritability, loss of libido and sexual drive, and difficulty concentrating. Problems like difficulty sleeping can also contribute to burnout (Hill and Curran 2016).

Burnout is a psychological state that can develop slowly over time. Many of the causes of burnout come from the workplace context: unfair treatment at work, excessive workload, lack of clarity in your role, lack of management support, and chronic time pressure (Maslach and Leiter 2016). Having perfectionistic expectations of yourself will make you much more likely to reach burnout than someone who sets more reasonable expectations. Could you be experiencing burnout? Check any of the symptoms listed below that apply to you.

☐ Finding your job increasingly stressful and frustrating

☐ Feeling cynical about your work, the work environment, or your colleagues

☐ Getting physical symptoms such as headaches and stomachaches

☐ Feeling drained and exhausted

☐ Feeling less able to do your job well

☐ Having difficulty concentrating and focusing on your work

☐ Feeling unable to cope

Both burnout and chronic stress can have lasting negative psychological and physical health effects, and if this a problem for you, something needs to change. As you work through the remaining chapters of this book, I encourage you to seek out opportunities to find calm, slow down the pace of your life, address issues that could be contributing to your stress, and make your health a greater focus. You may also benefit from professional support to help you develop strong boundaries, greater job clarity, skills in managing your managers, or potentially navigate a change in career.

Perfectionism Can Hurt Your Relationships

Perfectionism causes problems in relationships of all kinds. You may work so hard that your relationships suffer or find yourself married to your work rather than in a loving relationship. You may worry about how you look or what you say, stopping you from deeply connecting with others. Perhaps, you find it hard to take a risk to start a new relationship altogether. After all, what if it doesn't work out? You might also worry about how other people see you and believe you are not good enough for your partner, friends, or colleagues. Plagued by self-doubt, you may crave reassurance, but it's never enough.

Expecting perfection from others will also cause friction and conflict. People may find you nit-picky, difficult to please, and critical. They may never feel good enough for you, and sometimes, this leads to important relationships completely breaking down.

Consider how your perfectionism might affect your important relationships. Take a moment to complete the following sentences:

My perfectionism makes relationships more difficult when I _____

_____.

I often expect _____ of other people.

Activity: Assessing the Quality of Your Relationships

This activity is a chance to do an audit of your current relationships and evaluate which relationships are working well for you both, and where there might be tension, conflict, or disconnection. Below, I've listed eight broad types of relationships. Not all will be relevant to you. I've also included two blank rows for you to add any other relationships that deserve a special mention. Complete the table by checking the answer that best fits your experience of this relationship.

	Warm, close, connected	Friendly, comfortable	A little strained	Tense, distant, pressured	Broken, in conflict
Parents					
Brothers/Sisters					
Partner/Spouse					
Children					
Friends					
Colleagues/Peers					
Managers					
Employees/Staff					

	Warm, close, connected	Friendly, comfortable	A little strained	Tense, distant, pressured	Broken, in conflict

Relationships that are more tense, distant, or in conflict might be something you might aim to improve using the skills you learn in this book. I encourage you to look for opportunities to enhance the closeness and warmth in your important relationships as much as you can. Deeper, heartfelt relationships are likely to immeasurably improve your life. Of course, sometimes relationships with difficult people or long-term conflict cannot be fixed, and while this might be sad and hurtful, you need to make the decisions that are right for you. If you can't create warm connections with these people, work to strengthen your connections to other important people in your life.

Missing Out on the "Good Stuff" of Life

While some people tend to push toward perfectionistic standards with greater and greater urgency, others respond by pulling away from the things they fear. Once it becomes clear that you'll never meet your standards, it can become difficult to keep trying. Avoiding risks and feeling uncomfortable can cause you to miss so many important and enjoyable things. Check any that apply to you from the list below.

Have you missed:

☐ Work opportunities because you expect you won't do it well

☐ Meeting new people because you are worried you won't be liked

☐ Romantic relationships because you feel scared of being rejected

☐ Trying new things because you feel certain you will look silly or awkward

☐ Opportunities for learning because you were scared you would fail

☐ New hobbies because you don't have time in your day

☐ A work promotion because your extra effort isn't recognized, or because you struggle to get your work finished to your standards

As you work through the following chapters, you will have opportunities to move toward things you've been avoiding. I want you to experience all the richness and glorious messiness that life has to offer. To do this, you'll need to take some risks and lean into what makes you uncomfortable. But first, we need to finish taking stock of the losses. Motivation to change starts from this place of understanding.

Activity: What Is Your Perfectionism Really Costing You?

In this next activity, you'll look deeper into what your perfectionism has cost you. Read the following script before finding a quiet, peaceful place to complete this practice. Once again, if you struggle with visualization, read this through, take notes, and then quietly spend time considering your answers. Consider each set of questions with an attitude of openness and curiosity. An audio file of this activity can be found at http://www.newharbinger.com/48077.

Find a comfortable seated position and begin by noticing the feeling of your body resting on the chair. Noticing all the parts of your body that are touching the chair. Notice how your feet are resting on the floor. Let your body sink into the space. Close your eyes and practice Soothing Rhythm Breathing until you feel calm and at peace.

Start by considering your childhood.

Think about times when you behaved in unhelpful perfectionistic ways as a child. Imagine yourself when you were young, with your childlike worries about performing well, pleasing others, or being "good enough."

What would you avoid as a child because you were scared you might fail?

What opportunities might you have missed as a result?

Notice any emotions and physical sensations inside you as you think about your childhood in this way. Reflect on this for a minute or two before moving on to the next section.

Next, think about your adolescence and young adulthood.

Think about times when you might have behaved in a perfectionistic way. Imagine yourself as an adolescent, noticing your worries about doing well, or being a good student or friend.

What did you avoid because you feared not doing it well?

What opportunities might you have missed as a result?

Notice any emotions and physical sensations inside you as you think about your adolescence in this way. Reflect on this for a minute or two before moving on to the next section.

Finally, consider your adult life until now.

Think about times in your adult life when you have behaved in perfectionistic ways. Imagine yourself as you are now, at work, study, or in your relationships.

What do you avoid because you fear not doing it well?

What have you been avoiding since childhood that you are still avoiding now?

What opportunities might you have missed as a result?

Notice any emotions and physical sensations inside you as you think about your adult life in this way. Reflect on this for a minute or two.

Now take several long, deep breaths as you bring this activity to a gentle close. Allow a feeling of calm to develop within your body. Feel yourself sitting, with feet on the floor and your body on the chair. When you are ready, open your eyes and return to the day, taking this sense of calm with you.

Now, take a moment to consider the insights that have surfaced in this activity.

What has perfectionism cost you:

In your work or study?

_____

_____

In your relationships?

_____

_____

As a parent, guardian, or caregiver?

_____

_____

In your physical health?

_____

_____

In your leisure, sports, or creative pursuits?

_____

_____

In your home environment?

_____

_____

In your spiritual practice?

_____

_____

In your ability to help others?

_____

_____

By now, you may be starting to feel a little uncomfortable. It can be difficult to acknowledge that you've been doing things that cause you problems because this must mean you've made mistakes. Let me reassure you that there is a purpose to these activities. By exploring what you have lost, you can more clearly see where you might change things for the better.

Where Are These Habits Taking You?

Henry Ford famously said, "If you always do what you've always done, you'll always get what you've always got." Consider the rest of your life stretching out from here. If you continue as you are right now, how might your future pan out? Continuing with your unhelpful habits may have a devastating impact on your future contentment and life satisfaction.

Activity: Where Is Your Perfectionism Taking You?

In this activity, you'll have an opportunity to consider the potential influence of perfectionism on several major life milestones. As you read the following situations, note down your responses in the space provided. Focus on those milestones that are particularly relevant to you.

Being in a Loving Relationship

How might your perfectionism interfere with your ability to have a loving relationship?

_____

_____

How might your perfectionism disrupt how you feel in your relationship?

_____

_____

How might your perfectionism affect your partner?

_____

_____

Starting a Family and Being a Parent

How might your perfectionism influence your relationships with your children?

_____

_____

How might your perfectionism interfere with your enjoyment of being a parent?

_____

_____

How might your perfectionism influence your ability to support your children as they grow?

_____

_____

Going on an Overseas Vacation

How might your perfectionism disrupt your ability to plan and enjoy a vacation?

_____

_____

Getting Your First (or Next) Dream Job

How might your perfectionism interfere with your ability to flourish and succeed in this role?

_____

_____

Changing Your Career or Starting Your Own Business

How might your perfectionism affect your ability to do well in this new venture?

_____

_____

How might your perfectionism influence how much you enjoy this experience?

_____

_____

Finishing Work and Living in Retirement

How might your perfectionism make it more difficult to retire feeling satisfied?

_____

_____

How might your perfectionism influence how much you enjoy your retirement?

_____

_____

Your Final Years

How might your perfectionism interfere with your ability to enjoy your final years?

_____

_____

How might your perfectionism influence how you feel about your life?

_____

_____

By now, you might be feeling quite hopeless about the past *and* the future. You might even have thoughts like, "I really need to work harder to overcome these problems!" or "I should have managed things better!" If this sounds familiar, I encourage you to take a deep breath and notice these unhelpful perfectionistic thoughts for what they are. Let your feelings of doubt, confusion, and loss settle for a moment. Remember that you didn't choose to be struggling in this way, *and* you can still change where you are going.

Why Do You Keep Doing Things That Cause You Problems?

Why do you persist with your unhelpful perfectionistic habits when they are causing you so many problems? The following section may seem a little bit technical at points; however, I invite you to make the effort to read it because understanding the concepts will be helpful as you begin to tackle your unhelpful perfectionistic habits.

How Have You Developed These Unhelpful Habits?

Your habits did not come from just anywhere; they were learned and continue to occur because of what happens immediately after you do them. Whether you are aware of them, all behaviors have consequences of some kind. Your unhelpful perfectionistic habits have been rewarded in some way. Rewards can be something good that happens (positive reinforcement) or something bad going away (negative reinforcement). Positive reinforcements are often easy to see. If you study hard and get a good grade, your studying has been positively reinforced. Negative reinforcement happens when something unwanted is taken away or neutralized because of your actions. If you thoroughly check your work, your anxiety about making a mistake will go down and the checking is negatively reinforced.

These short-term rewards are much more powerful reinforcers than long-term consequences. Behaviors that are rewarded by immediate positive or negative reinforcement are more likely to persist even when there are long-term unwanted consequences. Many unhelpful perfectionistic habits follow this pattern: unhelpful perfectionistic behaviors are rewarded because they lessen the risk of something bad happening (a mistake) in the short term. By doing so, these habits reduce uncomfortable feelings such as anxiety and shame. The unhelpful habit then persists even though in the long term the behavior causes bigger problems (Slade and Owens 1998). Let's look at how this works through some examples.

Juan had cystic fibrosis, a progressive genetic disease that required him to complete many daily treatments at home. If he did these properly, they took nearly an hour and resulted in coughing, shortness of breath, wheezing, and occasionally even vomiting. Juan knew that by doing these treatments, he was making his best efforts to improve his health and lengthen his lifespan. Juan knew he should do the treatments every day, yet he struggled to maintain this habit. Juan felt ashamed and guilty for not doing his treatments. He worried he was letting himself, his family, and the medical team down. Each time he started doing his treatments then stopped again, he felt hopeless. He wondered what was wrong with him. Eventually, Juan gave up trying to do his treatments at all. He started lying to his doctors, hiding his medical equipment from his family, and hoping no one found out. By doing so, he could ignore his health problems for much of the day and felt better, at least for a little while.

By avoiding his treatment, Juan was able to avoid uncomfortable feelings of guilt and shame in the short term. Not doing his treatment was being negatively reinforced even though the long-term costs were clear.

Procrastination is an unhelpful perfectionistic habit that is often rewarded in the short term, but in the long term, it causes many problems. In this next example, we explore how this works.

In his first year of college studying law, Simon felt anxious and uncertain. He worried he was not as smart as the other students, that he would fail his assignments, and that the work would be too hard. As the semester progressed, his fear of failing intensified. Simon would struggle to finish his work and hand it in on time. Whenever he got a new assignment, he put it off until later instead, watching Netflix and scrolling through social media late into the night. By distracting himself, he could forget about his worries for a while. Unfortunately, his assignments began to build up and the workload became unmanageable. Simon ended up dropping out, believing that he was not smart enough to be a lawyer because he couldn't do the work.

Simon's procrastination was reinforced in the short term because it offered him relief from his anxious feelings. The short-term relief from feeling anxious was a more immediate and powerful reinforcer for Simon's behavior than the longer-term risk of failing altogether.

Activity: Mapping Your Rewards and Consequences

In this activity, you'll have an opportunity to explore how short-term consequences reinforce your unhelpful perfectionistic habits.

Start by briefly describing a particularly unhelpful perfectionistic habit you've developed.

_____

_____

_____

_____

What are the short-term rewards for this behavior?

(What uncomfortable feelings or outcomes are taken away when you do this?)

_____

_____

_____

_____

What are the unwanted consequences in the long term?

_____

_____

_____

_____

Unhelpful perfectionistic habits usually try to remove some unwanted internal uncomfortable experience such as fear, shame, or embarrassment and an unwanted event such as making a mistake. If you've been trying to control how you feel through these habits, it is destined to fail.

Control Is the Problem, Not the Solution

There are many aspects of your world you can directly control. You can turn on the air conditioner when it is hot and put on a sweater when it is cold. You can also avoid making mistakes by looking out for them and taking evasive action.

Examples of Things You Can Control

Fixing your car when it's broken (if you have the money)

Working hard on your assignment

Choosing to eat nutritious food

Going for a walk

Deciding what to watch on TV

Choosing the snacks that you eat in front of the TV

Deciding whether to get a dog or a cat

Being kind to people

Avoiding mistakes that you can foresee

Since you have gained success by controlling the world around you, it is natural to assume you can control your internal world the same way. At first glance, it seems like you can control things like being hungry, thirsty, or tired. After all, you can go to bed early when you are tired, eat when you are hungry, and drink when you are thirsty. However, you are not actually controlling these sensations, you are *responding* to them. So really, *the sensations are controlling you.*

Many people believe that they must control their thoughts and feelings. Each day you are bombarded by messages saying that you need to "think positive," "be motivated," or "feel happy" as if this was a choice. But how possible is this really? Check with your own experience. Have you tried to think positively and found all your "negative" thoughts went away? Sadly, many people feel as if they have failed because they haven't been able to make themselves happy with this approach (Walser 2019). Yet truthfully, *it just doesn't work.*

In reality, you have little influence over your thoughts, emotions, and inner physical sensations. Initially, you may not be sure this is true. On the following pages are a series of experiments that will allow you to evaluate for yourself how much control you have over your inner experiences. Try these out to discover for yourself what happens when you try to control your internal world.

Experiment: Can You Control Your Body's Physical Sensations?

Part 1:

Get up off your chair or lounge and run on the spot for twenty seconds. Knees high! Up, up, up!

Is your heart beating faster after doing this?

Now do it again, but this time, don't allow your heart to beat any faster. Can you do this? Most people would say it's ridiculous to suggest so. We cannot control our physiological responses in this way.

Part 2:

Which of these situations would you find most frightening?

1.   Skydiving for the first time

2.   Public speaking in front of an audience of one thousand of your peers

3.   Holding a live tarantula in your hand

Close your eyes and imagine you must do this exact thing *tomorrow*. How would you feel? Imagine the exact moment where you are about to step out of the plane, onto the stage, or hold out your hand to take the spider. What sensations would you notice in your body? Circle any that might apply, and add any other sensations to the end of the list.

agitated	exhausted	sweaty
anxious	flat	tense
choked up	frozen	tight
churned up	heavy	tired
clenched	numb	unsettled
deflated	on edge	weary
drained	restless	worked up
dulled	shaky	_____
empty	sick/nauseous	_____

I invite you to check your own experience once again. How much control would you have over what happened inside your body in that moment? Could you choose to stop your hand from shaking, your stomach from churning, or your heart from beating fast? Rate how much control you would have over your internal physical sensations below.

No
Control

Complete
Control

| 1 | 2 | 3 | 4 | 5 | 6 | 7 | 8 | 9 | 10 |

Many people expect themselves to be able to control how they feel in challenging situations. Yet, how reasonable is it to expect yourself to stay calm in situations where you feel anxious or afraid? Fear can trigger involuntary physical reactions that you simply can't control. Do you let these uncomfortable sensations stop you from doing things?

Experiment: Can You Control Your Emotions?

Part 1:

Try this famous experiment and see what happens. Put this book down, walk out into the street, and fall in love with the very first stranger you see. I mean, *really* fall in love with them. Notice the quickening of your heart each time you see them. Feel that warm glow as you look into their eyes.

How did this go? Were you successful in falling in love? If I were to pay you a million dollars, would you be any more successful? Truthfully?

Part 2:

For the next two minutes, think about a situation that usually makes you angry. Imagine the situation in vivid detail. While you do this, make sure you *do not* feel any anger at all.

Were you able to turn off this emotion? Rate how much direct control you have over your emotions below.

No
Control

Complete
Control

| 1 | 2 | 3 | 4 | 5 | 6 | 7 | 8 | 9 | 10 |

Sometimes you might soothe difficult, uncomfortable emotions by taking deep breaths or receiving a hug. Sometimes you might cheer yourself up by watching something funny that makes you laugh. However, this is you *responding* to your emotions, not controlling them. You may have developed some helpful and unhelpful ways of responding to your emotions.

Experiment: Can You Control Your Thoughts?

Read the following statements silently and see what your mind does.

Twinkle, twinkle little _____

Three blind mice, see how they _____

Practice makes _____

You might have noticed your mind finishing these statements all by itself. Now, read the following sentences, and this time *don't* let your mind finish them. Do not think about what the missing word might be.

You can't judge a book by its _____

Have your _____ and eat it too

Time flies when you're having _____

How did you do?

How much control do you have over your thoughts? Rate your response below.

No   Complete
Control   Control

| 1 | 2 | 3 | 4 | 5 | 6 | 7 | 8 | 9 | 10 |

It turns out that it is remarkably difficult, and maybe even impossible to control our thoughts. You can distract yourself, keep busy, and try to think of something else, but this is not the same as controlling your thinking. Trying to control your thoughts is likely to be wasted effort.

Experiment: Can You Control Your Imagination?

Read the following passage and follow the instructions as best you can.

Right now, do not think about eating a warm, gooey, chocolate-filled donut. Don't imagine holding the warm donut in your hand. Don't imagine the sweet sensation of the sugary dough on your lips as you bite down. Whatever you do, don't visualize the chocolate filling oozing out into your mouth as you take that warm, sweet first bite. Mmmmmm…

How did you do? Could you completely avoid imagining those warm donuts?

You might be able to distract yourself for a while, but eventually you'll become aware that you are not imagining chocolate donuts and *wham*, there it is—you are thinking about chocolate donuts.

How much control do you have over your imagination? Rate your response below.

No   Complete
Control   Control

1	2	3	4	5	6	7	8	9	10

Perhaps, you enjoyed those images as much as I did. Maybe you even started to salivate like me. Just to be sure, you might like to try this experiment on a friend too. Read the activity aloud and see what happens. I think you will find that you have little control over your imagination.

Take a moment now to look back over what happened in these experiments. How much direct control do you have over your thoughts, emotions, and physical sensations? I suspect the answer is "not much." You can *respond* to your internal world (eat when you are hungry, breathe deeply to calm your nerves, or distract yourself from unwanted thoughts), but you can't directly *control* it.

Examples of Things You Can't Control

Weather

Accidents and bad luck

How other people feel about us

What other people say about us

Our thoughts and mental images

Our emotions

Our internal physical sensations

So, if you can't control these things, is it possible that you are wasting your time by trying? Once again, check your own experience. What has happened to your uncomfortable feelings like fear, anxiety, and tension while you've been trying not to feel this way? Circle the answer that fits best:

I have been getting fewer uncomfortable feelings

I have been getting the same number of uncomfortable feelings

I have been getting more of the uncomfortable feelings

Usually, when you try to get rid of your uncomfortable feelings, sensations, and thoughts of failure, the feelings end up getting more intense *and* more frequent. Surely, there must be a better way.

Stop Hiding from Discomfort

The first step toward building more helpful perfectionistic habits is being able to accommodate the uncomfortable feelings that come with mistakes and failure, instead of trying to control them. I know this sounds counterintuitive. I appreciate that this is a leap of faith and you might need to trust me here. I am asking you to allow yourself to feel more of these experiences rather than avoiding them. Learning to recognize, label, and allow yourself to experience these uncomfortable feelings will give you a greater ability to hold your course and take steps toward what is important. The place to start is by learning to notice and label your unwanted inner experiences.

Activity: Noticing and Labeling Your Inner Experiences

The next activity is a mindfulness exercise that will take you about five to seven minutes, or longer if you choose. Find a quiet, peaceful place to complete the activity. An audio file can be found at http://www.newharbinger.com/48077.

Before you start, think of something you would normally avoid doing such as public speaking, asking for feedback, or singing in public. Write down your example here:

_____

_____

Place your feet squarely on the ground and sit so that your back is straight and your head feels supported on your shoulders. Close your eyes and practice Soothing Rhythm Breathing for several minutes until you are in a calm and reflective space.

Think about the situation you've chosen. Imagine yourself doing this task. Develop a rich and detailed picture of the situation, what you are doing, and who you are with. Engage all your senses, noticing anything you hear, smell, taste, or touch. Take two to three minutes to imagine yourself in this way.

As if you are a scientist who is gathering vital information, watch what happens to your internal world when you think about doing this challenging task. Observe how your body feels without trying to change your experience.

Notice any emotions that are bubbling up right now. Remember, you can have many emotions at one time, so find and label as many different ones as you can. Perhaps you feel tense, on edge, uncertain, or uneasy. Pay particular attention to the uncomfortable physical sensations that show up alongside these emotions. Notice where these sensations can be found inside your body. Take several minutes to explore this within yourself. Slow down and take your time.

Your mind will wander. Minds have a habit of doing this. So, try to catch yourself thinking. Notice any thoughts including judgments, evaluations, doubts, or worries as they pass through your mind. Allow yourself time to notice the many different thoughts your mind generates in this situation. You may even notice thoughts like, "I can't do this properly" or "This is confusing." Watch all these thoughts as they drift by.

Finally, take one long, slow, deep breath. Then, in your own time, leave this situation behind and gently return to feeling your feet resting on the floor. Feel your body resting on the chair. When you are ready, return to the room and open your eyes. Stretch.

Congratulations, you've just completed a short mindfulness activity. If you have never done this before, you may find it difficult to concentrate at first. Remember your mindfulness skills will develop with repeated practice. Even with lots of practice, sometimes our minds just don't want to focus! You can develop your skills in mindfulness further by using the many apps available online.

Take a few minutes to note down your observations. First, circle any *emotions* listed that you noticed during the activity, adding anything missing to the end of the list. Remember, you may feel many different things at the same time.

alone	grief	tearful
angry	guilty	tired
anxious	helpless	uneasy
ashamed	hopeless	unsure
confused	hurt	upset
defeated	invisible	useless
dejected	isolated	victimized
disconnected	lonely	worried
disgusted	motivated	worthless
distracted	neutral	_____
doubtful	overwhelmed	_____
embarrassed	powerless	_____
fearful	regretful	_____
foolish	resentful	
frustrated	sad	

Then, circle any of the *physical sensations* that you experienced during this activity, adding anything else to the end of the list.

agitated	exhausted	sweaty
anxious	flat	tense
choked up	frozen	tight
churned up	heavy	tired
clenched	numb	unsettled
deflated	on edge	weary
drained	restless	worked up
dulled	shaky	_____
empty	sick/nauseous	_____

The transition toward more helpful perfectionism will involve trying new things, stumbling, messing up, and changing direction; in other words, putting yourself into uncomfortable situations and trying things you are not good at. This means that at any time, the uncomfortable internal sensations and emotions that have emerged in this activity could show up. Be prepared, and don't let these feelings stop you. Instead, think about how you will respond when things get difficult; when the new skills you will be trying are hard. If you walk away, withdraw, and decide you can't make these changes, what might you lose?

Putting It Together

Your perfectionism developed to ensure success and avoid failure; however, in the end, it's caused more problems than it's solved. It is likely that your perfectionism has cost you a great deal. You will continue to make these losses for as long as you continue the same habits that got you here. Perfectionistic habits, like procrastinating, checking, or working harder, provide you with some short-term relief from your fears, but they have a long-term cost. If you look think back over your life, it's unlikely your fears have gone away by doing this. In fact, your unhelpful loops have probably made your fear worse over time.

Trying to control your anxious feelings is an understandable response. Yet, it also causes the problems you seek to avoid. In short, it doesn't work. You need an approach that can help you live a life full of purpose and intention. This starts with being able to notice and label your inner experiences, thoughts, emotions, and sensations. This will help you develop flexible ways of coping with challenges—and make more helpful choices.

Taking Small, Imperfect Steps: Your Personal Action Plan

Take a few minutes to create your Personal Action Plan for this chapter.

What did you learn in this chapter that was relevant to you?

1. _____

2. _____

3. _____

What did you learn about yourself?

1. _____

2. _____

3. _____

Over the coming days, what small actions would you be willing to take toward a life where your perfectionism is more helpful for you?

1. _____

2. _____

3. _____

CHAPTER 4

Building a Life You Love

Make room for the real important stuff.

—Tigger, from *Christopher Robin: The Little Book of Pooh-isms*

In his famous song "Beautiful Boy (Darling Boy)," John Lennon sang about how even though we make plans for ourselves, life just keeps happening to us all the same. My hope is that through the steps you take in this book, your life does not "just happen" to you. I'd like you to experience a life that feels fulfilling. This kind of life is not about being busy and checking off our goals; it's where you feel deeply satisfied by the contribution that you've made to others and spend time doing things that add to your life in substantial ways.

Perfectionism keeps you busy. It pushes you to achieve more, or avoid the things that scare you. Your perfectionistic habits might protect you from failure, but they probably don't fill your life with joy. Unfortunately, stopping your perfectionistic habits is not enough to create a life that enriches you—you must replace your unhelpful behaviors with purposeful action in the direction of things that are important to you even though it means moving closer to your fears and your desire to hide or escape (Walser 2019).

Living a purposeful and fulfilling life takes deliberate, consistent, and purposeful action. It is an ongoing process where you move toward a life that you love, and something to which you must pay close attention for your entire life (Walser 2019). To achieve this, you need to know what you value and take deliberate, consistent steps toward those values.

In this chapter, you'll develop a rich picture of what would be a rewarding and fulfilling life for *you*; a future that is so satisfying when you think about it, your eyes glisten and heart feels light. I bet you already know some of the ingredients of this life. Capture these now by completing the following sentence.

A life that was meaningful and fulfilling for me would include _____, _____, and _____.

So, why aren't you living a life that you love now? Before you go any further in this chapter, take this opportunity to explore how you might be getting off track. Perhaps, you get stuck being busy, chasing achievements and "success." Or, you get railroaded into doing what you believe you *should* do and what others expect of you. As you explore these in more detail, think about whether you have fallen into these traps at some point, and if they are still getting in your way today.

Living Life as What You Achieve or Attain

When you think about your future, do you focus on the things you'd like to achieve? Do you strive for more money, higher grades, a nice car, a grand house, a beautiful wedding, or a high-status job, yet continue to feel unfulfilled? These are the kinds of goals that Western culture suggests will make us happy, yet they can leave us dissatisfied. After all, once you achieve your goal, what do you do next? You can be so busy reaching goals that you miss richer, more satisfying aspects of life.

As he reached his late thirties, William realized he'd spent years focusing on financial success. He owned a luxury imported car, a huge house with a yard, and a boat that remained moored because he never had the time to go fishing. William had worked hard, traveling every week to see clients, close deals, and earn big bonuses. Late nights and long client lunches had taken a toll on his health and relationships. He'd broken up with his girlfriend and rarely saw his friends, most of whom had young families and busy lives. At a Sunday lunch, William's mother looked him over and asked him "Are you happy?" He did not know what to say. William knew that something huge was missing in his life, but he didn't know how to make things better.

William had spent years on a treadmill, working his way toward success, but the end result was a life that felt meaningless and empty. Do you focus on achieving new goals and getting things done? Complete the following questions by circling either Yes or No:

Whenever I achieve something, I set a new goal for myself right away.   Y / N

I structure my days around the tasks I must complete.   Y / N

I believe I must always achieve the goals I set for myself.   Y / N

When I achieve something, I move on quickly and don't celebrate.   Y / N

After I achieve a goal, I don't feel satisfied.   Y / N

When I focus on achieving my goals, I tend to neglect my relationships.   Y / N

If you answered yes to several of the questions above, your focus on achievement might be at the expense of your greater well-being. Something needs to change.

Doing What You Should, Not What You Love

When you were young, important adults in your life probably helped guide your direction. Your parents, grandparents, teachers, religious leaders, and other adults told you what to do, and probably for the most part, you did it. In adulthood, you set your own path and built your life based upon what you learned in childhood. You may still be doing what others expect of you today, or perhaps you went the other way and did exactly the opposite. No one hands you a rule book when you are born that tells you how to live your life well. Instead, you listen to the advice provided by those around you. Not understanding your own priorities can leave you feeling confused, disappointed, resentful, or lost as though there's something important missing in your life.

> Eliza had always achieved what she strived for. She'd worked hard at school and was now at college, studying law. Her parents were happy; after all, they were both lawyers too. Every semester, she worked hard to get good grades, then over summer, she went home and helped in her parents' business. As the years went by, Eliza began to feel disenchanted. Life had become dull and repetitive, and the future seemed mapped out and predictable. Eliza didn't want to live her parents' lives, and she began to look elsewhere for adventure. When new friends invited her to parties off campus, Eliza started experimenting with pills and drinking, letting off steam from her mundane life. This filled a gap for Eliza, and she began to feel as if she was having fun at last.

Eliza was following in her parents' footsteps without fully considering what she wanted to do. Do you ever feel trapped working toward someone else's priorities, doing what you think you *should* do? Complete the following questions by circling either Yes or No:

I feel trapped into doing things I don't really enjoy   Y / N

I focus on doing what others expect of me   Y / N

It is essential to do the right thing   Y / N

I have always done what my parents or teachers think I should   Y / N

I have not questioned the path I've taken in life   Y / N

If you've answered yes to several of the items above, you have been pulled away from experiencing your life as something enriching and deeply rewarding. Instead, you are going through the motions, doing what you think you *should* do.

The rest of this chapter will help you uncover your values. Understanding this will not give you a road map that tells you exactly what to do, but it will give you a compass so you can tell when you are heading in the right direction—and when you are getting off track. Knowing your values will enable you to set a clearer, more purposeful direction toward a fulfilling life.

What Are Values?

Your values are statements that describe what you want to stand for, what's important, and how you want to live your life. Values must be freely chosen and must feel right to you, *and no one else* (J. Stoddard 2019), and as such, cannot be wrong (Tirch et al. 2019). This means that while your parents, friends, cultural heritage, or religion might influence your values, they do not define them. Your values are neither who you are "supposed to be" in the eyes of others nor are they the same as morals, although you may value living in ways that are consistent with your faith such as with compassion and acceptance.

Values are something that *you do* as well as being a quality you can embody as a person (Hayes and Smith 2005). If you value being kind, you can show this by being thoughtful and considerate in your interactions with other people. If you value being loving, it's something you can express by being warm and caring to others. Remember, your values are something that *you* do. You cannot rely on others for your values, which means that you cannot value "being loved" or "being treated with respect," because you need other people to do these things.

Some people try to define their values using abstract concepts such as "integrity," "courage," or "authenticity." These can sound more like corporate slogans than personal values and aren't always helpful because they don't tell you how, when, and with whom you'd like to live these values. It can be more useful to describe your values using brief sentences. Authenticity might become "being honest about myself with friends." Integrity could be "speaking and acting consistently and with consideration for others." Courage might be better described as "saying or doing what is important, even when it is uncomfortable."

Values are quite different from goals because, unlike goals, values cannot ever be checked off as complete. You *live* your values, not finish them. If you value being in a loving relationship, there are many tasks you can perform as part of this, such as taking your partner out to dinner, buying them thoughtful gifts, or spending time listening to their concerns. However, the loving relationship is not *completed* by any of these steps. Neither is it completed by moving in together or getting married. It's *how* you approach the relationship that matters; being loving is the principle that you keep living through your actions, and defines the tasks and goals that are important to you in your relationship.

In the next section, you are going to explore your values through a series of self-reflective questions. The domains have been inspired by the Valued Living Questionnaire (Wilson and DuFrene 2008; Wilson and Murrell 2004) and include questions about your relationships, work, education, personal growth, health, hobbies and leisure, home life and environment, spirituality and religious practice, citizenship, and helping others. As you step through the process, feel free to let your mind roam across all these areas of your life, even if you have never actively considered them before. Inside your wondering could be undiscovered gems.

We Hurt Where We Care

Before you complete this next section, I need to prepare you. Exploring your values can be a little challenging at times. As Steven Hayes, one of the co-developers of Acceptance and Commitment Therapy, once said, "We hurt where we care, and we care where we hurt." If your unhelpful habits are taking you away from a life that is meaningful to you, looking at your values can be an uncomfortable experience. You may find yourself thinking, "Why haven't I being doing this already?" or "Why have I been wasting so much time?" If these thoughts show up, I encourage you to pause. In this exact moment lies an opportunity to be kind to yourself. With this in mind, let's get started.

Getting to the Heart of Your Life

Over the following pages is a three-step process that will help you expand your thinking and tease out common themes. Pay close attention to the aspects of your life that are essential for you *beyond* achieving goals and gaining recognition. Remember to tune in to what feels right for *you* as you work through this process.

Step 1: Find the Keys to Yourself

Our first step will develop a rich picture of what is meaningful for you through a guided interview. In each step, base your answers on what you would do if you were being the best version of yourself. Look for words that feel heartfelt, raw, and a little inspiring. Describe the personal qualities that you would like to demonstrate as you pursue important things in your life. If you see yourself as a hard worker, do you value being thoughtful, thorough, and persistent in your work? If you would like to be a "good mom" or "good dad," do you aim to be loving, patient, kind, and playful with your kids? Here is a list of personal qualities to inspire you in your answers.

Personal Qualities That People Value

adventurous	fun	playful
appreciative	funny	positive
approachable	generous	powerful
attentive	giving	present
balanced	healthy	productive
calm	helpful	reliable
caring	honest	respectful
compassionate	honoring	risk-taking
connected	humorous	self-sufficient
consistent	imaginative	sensual
courageous	independent	serene
creative	inspirational	spiritual
curious	intimate	spontaneous
disciplined	intuitive	stable
encouraging	kind	strong
energetic	loving	structured
enthusiastic	loyal	supportive
expressive	non-judgmental	thorough
fair	nurturing	thoughtful
faithful	open	tolerant
focused	organized	understanding
forgiving	patient	warm
free	peaceful	wise
friendly	persistent	witty

As you complete this activity, pay particular attention to the ideas that resonate and energize you. You do not need to find the perfect words, as this will get you bogged down. So instead, for now, generate a description using as many words as you can. You will have a chance to narrow down your answers later.

Also, not all the questions that follow will equally apply to you. Perhaps, you are not a parent or currently working. For these questions, think about situations that share similar qualities. If you have retired from paid work, think about how you approach activities like hobbies or volunteering. If you don't have children, think about how you might approach future parenthood or consider your relationships with children as a brother, sister, cousin, aunt, uncle, or godparent.

Now, if you are ready, begin with something that always sits at the heart of a valued life: your relationships.

Relationships

The Dalai Lama once tweeted, "From the first day of our life until our last breath, the very foundation of our existence is affection and human warmth." Loving relationships and connections with others seem to be at the heart of a life well-lived. Using the personal qualities listed earlier as inspiration, answer the following questions.

What personal qualities would you like to express when you are with your family?

_____

_____

How would you like to be when you are with your intimate partner?

_____

_____

What kind of parent would you like to be?

_____

_____

What kind of person would you like to be when with your friends?

_____

_____

When you are with difficult people or in situations of conflict, how would you like to express your views?

_____

_____

How would you like to behave toward strangers and other acquaintances?

_____

_____

Now, using the words and phrases above as a guide, complete the following sentences.

I would like to be _____, _____, and _____ when I'm with the people I care for most.

I would like to be _____, _____, and _____ when I'm with my friends.

I would like to be _____, _____, and _____ in situations of conflict or with difficult people.

I would like to be a mother or father who is _____, _____, and _____ with my kids.

I would like to treat all people with _____ and _____.

Work and Achievement

Finding satisfaction and enjoyment in your work is something that contributes greatly to a fulfilling and enriching life. Here is a list of qualities and attributes that can be found in rewarding work. As you complete the following questions, consider whether any of these qualities would be highly valued by you.

autonomy and self-direction	intellectual challenge
caring for animals	job security
challenging (and achievable) work	leadership opportunities
clearly defined tasks	leadership that is consistent and supportive
collaboration and teamwork	learning and growth
complex problem-solving	managing others
connecting to a higher purpose	working outdoors
creative and/or artistic expression	pleasant working environment
exacting and precise work	social connections with colleagues
feedback and recognition	solving technical problems
financial rewards	addressing social and environmental issues
flexibility and choice	supportive colleagues
fun	teaching
helping others	teamwork
independent work	wide variety of tasks

What do you find satisfying or fulfilling in your current area of work?

_____

_____

What would make your work more meaningful for you?

_____

_____

What kinds of tasks or activities would you do in your dream job?

_____

_____

What personal qualities would you like to express in your work?

_____

_____

What kinds of work achievements give you the greatest personal satisfaction?

_____

_____

Now complete the following sentences:

A career where I can _____ would be satisfying and fulfilling.

I particularly enjoy work where I can _____.

When I achieve _____, I feel

_____.

Education and Personal Growth

It is through the learning you do over your lifetime that you get closer to being the best possible version of yourself. Learning can come in many forms including through your work, study, new experiences, or relationships.

What knowledge or skill would you most like to learn?

Consider different languages, technical skills, creative, or expressive activities.

_____

_____

What is it about gaining this knowledge or skill that you would appreciate?

_____

_____

What adventures or new experiences do you dream of having in your lifetime?

Consider travel, learning new skills, being independent, starting new relationships, or parenthood. Note down any dreams or adventures you wish you could have, no matter whether they are achievable right now.

_____

_____

_____

Now complete the following sentences:

I am inspired to learn more about _____.

It is important to me to experience _____ in my life.

Health and Physical Well-Being

How you look after your health and physical body supports your ability to live a valued life. Yet, many of us struggle to be consistent with health routines and self-care.

What habits would you like to change to improve your health?

Consider habits such as diet, exercise, smoking, drinking, medications, and sleep.

_____

_____

What will you be able to do with greater and long-lasting health?

Consider things such as looking after your children or grandchildren, traveling, or enjoying hobbies or sports.

_____

_____

Now complete the following:

It is important to look after my health and well-being because this will enable me to

_____.

Hobbies and Leisure

Mahatma Gandhi once said, "There is more to life than increasing its speed." Beyond work and the essentials of daily life, it is your hobbies and interests that allow you to explore new, creative, and adventurous parts of yourself. Leisure time not only allows you to recharge your batteries but also allows you to broaden, develop, and enrich your life in many ways.

What new hobbies, skills, sports, or leisure activities would you most like to learn?

_____

_____

What kinds of activities help you to relax and unwind?

_____

_____

When you are fully engaged in your hobbies, how do you feel?

_____

_____

Now complete the following sentences:

Valued activities that inspire and energize me are _____, _____ , and _____.

These activities give me opportunities to express the personal qualities of _____, _____ , _____, and _____.

Home and Environment

Both our natural world and the smaller world you create inside your home are crucial to how you feel. You can create environments for yourself that make you feel energized and at ease.

Thinking beyond objects and possessions, how do you like your home to feel?

Consider aspects of your home environment such as coziness, comfort, space to yourself, somewhere to be alone, room to be creative, organization, orderliness, access to open spaces, nature, and safety.

_____

_____

What kinds of natural or urban environments do you enjoy spending time in?

_____

_____

How could you make the environments you spend time in more nurturing, rewarding, safe, and inspiring?

_____

_____

Now complete the following sentence:

I feel nurtured in environments that are _____, _____, and _____.

Spirituality and Religious Practice

Developing a spiritual practice takes effort and persistence over the long term and deep reflection on how you live your life. Spirituality involves developing the same personal qualities we appreciate in others such as gratitude, openness, generosity, self-compassion, and forgiveness.

What aspects of your spiritual practice nurture and sustain you?

_____

_____

What personal strengths would you like to develop through your spiritual practice?

_____

_____

Now complete the following sentence:

I would like to express the personal qualities of _____, _____, and _____ in my spiritual practice.

Citizenship and Helping Others

We can all contribute to our community, society, and environment in positive ways. While we might often focus on big contributions made by high-profile people, small actions taken by everyday people *every day* have a big effect too.

What local and global issues concern you the most?

Consider issues such as poverty, health, discrimination, climate change, environmental waste, water conservation, food sustainability, extremism, health care, and global conflict.

_____

_____

_____

How might you help make the world a better place through your actions?

Consider how you could make your small positive impact as a citizen of the world such as recycling, reducing waste, caring for disadvantaged people, or speaking up against discrimination.

_____

_____

_____

In what ways could you help the people, local community, or environment around you?

Consider the small steps you could take such as being a loving influence on your family, being a kind and caring friend, reducing waste, caring for animals, cleaning up your neighborhood, building relationships with your neighbors, or supporting local stores.

_____

_____

_____

Before you move on to the next step, take a moment to look back over all your responses so far. Circle the key words or phrases that resonate for you—the ones that touch your heart. How do you feel when you think about living your life in this way?

_____

_____

_____

Step 2: Look Back from the End of Your Life

This next step invites you to consider how you might feel in the later years of your life. By looking at your life from this perspective, you can better appreciate what gives your life meaning now (Walser 2019). You can also see the implications that your actions today, both big and small, will have if you continue making the same choices throughout your life.

So, imagine you have reached the final days of your life. As you look back over the years, what would you like to be able to say about the way you've lived?

_____

_____

_____

With whom would you have shared the most special moments?

_____

_____

_____

What legacy would you like to leave behind for others?

_____

_____

_____

In what ways would you have helped people during your life?

_____

_____

_____

The following question might feel confrontational; however, it is worth taking the time to answer.

How would you like people to remember you after you have died? I doubt this would be "bought a big house," "got lots of work done," or "stayed thin." Write down what you would like to be written on your tombstone below.

"Here lies _____, who _____

_____

_____."

Now, before you move on, take a moment to read back over all your answers to Step 2 and circle the key words that reflect the elements of a rewarding and fulfilling life for you.

Step 3: Pan for Gold: Sift Out What's Important

Now it's time to put your thoughts and reflections together. Look back over your answers and the words or phrases you've circled. Then, for each domain in the table below, summarize any common themes using two or three brief statements.

Valued Domain	What's Important to Me (My Values)
Relationships: • Family • Friendships • Intimate partners • Parenting	
Work and Achievement	
Education and Personal Growth	
Health and Physical Well-Being	
Hobbies and Leisure	
Home and Environment	

Valued Domain	What's Important to Me (My Values)
Spirituality and Religious Practice	
Citizenship and Helping Others	

Activity: Finding the Heart of What Matters

This activity is an opportunity to deepen your understanding of what it feels like to live a valued life. Read over the following script, then find a comfortable and quiet place to complete this practice. Once again, if you find visualizing difficult, reread your answers to the earlier activities and then spend time contemplating what it would be like to live your life in line with these values. An audio file of this activity can be found at http://www.newharbinger.com/48077.

Sit in a comfortable position with your body resting on your chair and your feet resting on the floor. Let your hands rest gently in your lap. Allow yourself to sink gently into this space. Notice the gentle pull of gravity into the earth. Close your eyes or lower your gaze to the floor and practice Soothing Rhythm Breathing. Open your chest and allow your shoulders to soften.

Imagine that in about five years from now, you've largely resolved the problems you are struggling with today and are living a life that is aligned with your values. As if watching yourself in a silent movie, spend several minutes observing yourself as you move through your day. Notice where you choose to spend your time and who you are with. Watch how you are interacting with the people around you. Consider the warmth and care you feel for these people. Pay attention to how you are living your values through your work, study, or other activities. Notice each moment when you are in contact with your values.

Observe the way you would hold your body. Perhaps, your head is held high in a confident and open position and your shoulders are relaxed. Gently adjust your posture to match your future self. Notice how your body feels when you are living your life according to your values.

Notice the emotions that arise within you as you explore your valued future. Look beyond feelings of happiness—notice any feelings of contentment, satisfaction, motivation, purpose, or fulfillment. Feel the richness and satisfaction of a life lived this way.

Stay with these sensations and emotions for as long as you like. Then, when you are ready, let go of this experience and bring your attention back to your body seated in the chair. Feel your feet resting on the floor. Open your eyes, taking this awareness with you through the rest of your day.

When you think about your valued life, do you feel motivated and inspired? Does this life make you smile? Do you feel connected to what's important? If so, fantastic. You've found values that can define your direction through life. You'll come back to these through the rest of this book and, I hope, beyond.

Where Are You Going?

As you pay greater attention to your values, you will notice the times when you get off track. You might find yourself distracted by perfectionistic goals, lost in the details, or avoiding things that scare you. You may have already been drifting like this for some time. In the next activity, you will explore how consistently you are living your values in everyday life.

Self-Evaluation: Aligning to Your Values

For each valued domain, rate how important that domain is for you in your life right now. Then, circle the number that indicates how consistently you are living according to your values.

Valued Domain	Importance (1–10)	Living Inconsistently with My Values								Living Consistent with My Values
Family Relationships		1	2	3	4	5	6	7	8	9	10
Friendships		1	2	3	4	5	6	7	8	9	10
Intimate Relationships		1	2	3	4	5	6	7	8	9	10
Parenting		1	2	3	4	5	6	7	8	9	10

Valued Domain	Importance (1–10)	Living Inconsistently with My Values								Living Consistent with My Values
Work and Achievement		1	2	3	4	5	6	7	8	9	10
Education and Personal Growth		1	2	3	4	5	6	7	8	9	10
Health and Physical Well-being		1	2	3	4	5	6	7	8	9	10
Hobbies and Leisure		1	2	3	4	5	6	7	8	9	10
Home and Environment		1	2	3	4	5	6	7	8	9	10
Spirituality and Religious Practice		1	2	3	4	5	6	7	8	9	10
Citizenship and Helping Others		1	2	3	4	5	6	7	8	9	10

Which three domains are most important in your life right now?

1. _____

2. _____

3. _____

In which three domains are you living in a way that is most consistent with your values? Draw a star next to these. Notice if these are also important domains for you. These are your *strengths* and are likely to be areas of satisfaction in your life. The more important they are, the more satisfying they will feel. Briefly describe what you are doing well in these domains.

1. _____

2. _____

3. _____

In which three domains are you currently living most inconsistently with your values? Draw a checkmark next to these. Notice if these are also important domains for you. These are your *pain points* and are areas of dissatisfaction in your life. The more important this is to you, the greater the pain. Briefly describe what you are struggling with in these domains.

1. _____

2. _____

3. _____

Which three domains should be your biggest focus for change?

1. _____

2. _____

3. _____

Now, pause here for a moment and take a deep breath. Remember how I mentioned that thinking about values can be uncomfortable? Realizing how far you have drifted away from your values often brings up painful thoughts and feelings. Notice these inner experiences right now. Circle any of the emotions below that you might be experiencing, adding any others that are missing.

alone	grief	tearful
angry	guilty	tired
anxious	helpless	uneasy
ashamed	hopeless	unsure
confused	hurt	upset
defeated	invisible	useless
dejected	isolated	victimized
disconnected	lonely	worried
disgusted	motivated	worthless
distracted	neutral	_____
doubtful	overwhelmed	_____
embarrassed	powerless	_____
fearful	regretful	_____
foolish	resentful	_____
frustrated	sad	

Now, slow down and notice any physical sensations that come with these emotions. Circle any that you might be experiencing right now, adding anything else to the end of the list.

agitated	exhausted	sweaty
anxious	flat	tense
choked up	frozen	tight
churned up	heavy	tired
clenched	numb	unsettled
deflated	on edge	weary
drained	restless	worked up
dulled	shaky	_____
empty	sick/nauseous	_____

Take a few slow, deep breaths, and for several minutes, see if you can make room for all these inner experiences, both comfortable *and* uncomfortable before moving on. While you may feel angry, disappointed, or critical of your mistakes, right now you have an opportunity to be a little kinder and more understanding toward yourself. Self-compassion is a crucial part of managing your unhelpful perfectionism better, and in this next activity, you can start practicing this skill.

Taking the First Step

Living a life that is aligned with your values might feel a million miles away. It might even feel impossible to achieve. Yet, living a valued life is a *process* that involves taking small steps every day toward what's important. Here is a chance to start living according to your values by committing to taking one step toward things that are meaningful for you. Perhaps, you might call an old friend, take the afternoon off to go for a hike, help someone in your neighborhood, or start a small project that you've been putting off until later. Whatever it is, it should be some small *and* important action. Briefly describe this small step toward your values, and when you would do it.

_____

_____

_____

As you complete this task, notice how good doing something that is aligned with your values feels inside.

Putting It Together

Perfectionism keeps you busy chasing goals and avoiding mistakes. Yet, a meaningful and enriched life is not lived this way. Your unhelpful perfectionistic habits might help you avoid failure, but they don't lead to a life that you love.

Your values describe what you want to stand for and how you want to live your life. Your values are uniquely your own and not moral or religious principles. They might be influenced by others, but in the end are something that feels right to you alone. As statements of what is important to you, they cannot be wrong. Values must be something you can take action toward, yet they cannot be checked off like goals.

In this chapter, you've had an opportunity to explore your values from several perspectives. With this understanding, you may start to notice the times when your daily actions are inconsistent with your values. This might trigger feelings of loss and regret, so I hope you've taken time to be gentle with yourself.

Understanding your values will give you a direction in which to travel in life. To live a fulfilling and satisfying life, it is not enough to change your unhelpful habits. You will need to make daily choices to orient your life toward what you value, replacing unhelpful habits with valued actions. The rest of this book is about putting this into action.

Taking Small, Imperfect Steps: Your Personal Action Plan

Take a minute to create your Personal Action Plan for this chapter.

What did you learn in this chapter that was relevant to you?

1. _____
2. _____
3. _____

What did you learn about yourself?

1. _____
2. _____
3. _____

Over the coming days, what small actions would you be willing to take toward a life where your perfectionism is more helpful for you?

1. _____
2. _____
3. _____

CHAPTER 5

There Are No Quick Fixes

Be brave, be curious, be determined, overcome the odds. It can be done.

—Stephen Hawking, from *Brief Answers to the Big Questions*

Right now, you might feel heavily burdened by your unhelpful perfectionistic habits and worried about whether you'll be successful in changing them. This chapter will help you work out what really needs to change—and it might be less than you think. Dialing back your perfectionism by *just 10 percent* is usually enough to make perfectionism work better for you. Once you scale down your perfectionism into something more rightsized for your life, you get to keep the aspects of your perfectionism that are helpful to you.

At first, changing just 10 percent of your perfectionistic habits might not seem nearly enough. You may believe you need a complete overhaul to finally be "better." Pay close attention to this desire to "fix" yourself. Could this be a covert attempt to make yourself perfect? Here is the challenge that lies inside any attempt to change perfectionism: How do you work toward *not* being perfectionistic without trying to do this perfectly? How do you learn to accept the parts of yourself that aren't perfect? How can you become "imperfectly imperfect"?

Your first step is to recognize the good sides to your perfectionism, and that you do not need to fix everything. Much of what you do, in the right amounts and the right situations, could be helpful for you. Checking your work for errors will improve the quality of your writing, taking some time before you respond to an email can help you formulate a more thoughtful response, and practicing your presentation will make your performance smoother and more confident. In the following table, write down those helpful aspects of your perfectionism that you would like to keep and the unhelpful habits you might like to change. While you work to change the unhelpful habits, don't throw away these helpful aspects of perfectionism.

Helpful Aspects of My Perfectionism	Unhelpful Aspects of My Perfectionism
Things I don't want to change because they are generally helpful and don't cause me problems:	Things I would like to change because they cause me big problems:

How did completing this table go for you? It can be quite difficult to think about both the positive and negative aspects of your perfectionism. You may focus so much on the things that are wrong with you, you struggle to think of anything that works well. Take a closer look at what you've written down. Are the unhelpful aspects *always* a problem? Which things in the unhelpful column, if you did them a bit less often or in a different way, could actually be useful? Which things in the helpful column, if you do too much or at the wrong time, could be quite unhelpful? Any habit can be either helpful or unhelpful depending on whether you adjust what you do according to the situation. So, perhaps nothing needs to stop completely. Rather, you could evaluate the usefulness of your behavior in the moment and adjust your approach when needed.

Targeting Your Most Unhelpful Habits

A small number of unhelpful habits cause the bulk of your problems. These are the things you keep doing even when they aren't working for you because you fear failing or other people judging you. Focusing your efforts on changing these behaviors will have the biggest impact on your life. It will create a significant positive change that is achievable and sustainable in the long term.

Whenever humans are confronted by a threat, we instinctively behave in ways designed to neutralize or remove the threat. Professor Emily Sandoz at the University of Louisiana describes the way people respond to their fears as either "running, fighting, or hiding." You might be running from a mistake when you are procrastinating, fighting when you are working really hard to prevent a mistake from happening, or hiding when you avoid certain risky situations altogether.

In the following pages, I describe some of the common behaviors you'll see in unhelpful perfectionism. As you read, think about which of these unhelpful habits cause you the most headaches. Some are probably more of a problem than others, and some might not even trouble you at all.

Procrastination

Procrastination is a hallmark of perfectionism and can have a devastating effect on your performance, create enormous stress, and even lead to the failure you fear most. "Procrastination" is a widely used term. When I talk about procrastination, I don't mean the times you avoid something because you don't like it such as putting off doing the laundry or preparing your tax returns. I mean those times you postpone doing a task because you are scared you will fail, people will judge you harshly, or where you risk making a mistake. In these situations, by saying "I'll do it later," you are responding to an urge to avoid the shame of making a mistake. You get to side-step your fear for a little while until your deadline looms and the task becomes impossible to ignore. (If there's no deadline, it may never get done.) When the stress caused by not doing the task is greater than your fear of failing, you must either take action or give up altogether.

Now completing his final year at university, studying civil engineering, Xavier was due to draft his major thesis. He'd designed his study, conducted dozens of interviews, and analyzed his data. He had pages and pages of notes, but he just couldn't start writing the final document. Whenever Xavier sat down to work, he felt paralyzed, sick in his stomach, and his mind went blank. Xavier had always enjoyed gaming and began spending hours playing online with his friends, increasing his ranking, and mentoring other people. So, this is what he did. Whole days slipped by this way. Xavier would play until the early hours of the morning because whenever he stopped and thought about his thesis, he'd feel his chest tighten, heart start racing, and that sick feeling all over again.

Do you make a habit of putting things off until later? Briefly describe a situation where you procrastinate in unhelpful ways.

_____

_____

_____

_____

_____

Excessive Checking

Checking your work, appearance, or performance can be helpful. Proofreading a document is important if you want to avoid spelling or grammatical errors and ensure your reader will understand what you have written. Checking your appearance before you head to a job interview can help you feel confident that you look appropriately neat and professional. However, checking can get out of hand when you are trying to avoid making *any mistake at all*. This is because no matter how much checking you do, you can never feel completely certain something is good enough. In fact, the more you check something, the less certain you tend to become (van den Hout and Kindt 2004), which makes it easy to get stuck in a checking loop. Your checking can even start to look like a compulsion like with OCD.

Having recently graduated from business school with top marks, Felipe felt extremely proud of landing a job at a global management consulting firm. He joined a cohort of new graduates from all over the country who seemed confident and self-assured. Although outside Felipe presented a bright and bubbly personality, inside he felt afraid, certain they'd find out that he really didn't know what he was doing. Felipe stayed quiet in meetings because he was frightened of saying something wrong or stupid in front of the senior consultants. In an attempt to calm himself down and feel in control, Felipe focused on how he looked. He built up a wardrobe of expensive suits, shoes, ties, and other accessories, and checked his appearance throughout the day to make sure he always looked perfect, hip, professional, and polished. Felipe felt he must always look the part even if he didn't feel like he belonged. Unfortunately, he was spending more and more time checking and adjusting his appearance, and worrying about how he looked.

Do you get stuck in a cycle of checking? Briefly describe a situation where your checking is causing you problems.

_____

_____

_____

_____

_____

Working Too Hard

Working hard can often lead to higher quality outcomes and recognition from others. It can be so satisfying to absorb yourself in your work in this way. However, at some point, working hard doesn't add any more to the outcome. If you keep working hard to avoid mistakes, without seeing any greater results, you can end up feeling demoralized, drained, and burned out.

Emma loved working in the law. Her first job since graduating was as a junior lawyer in a global firm. She'd been involved in some big negotiations and worked for some demanding partners. Anxious to do a good job and prove herself, Emma began working longer and longer days. Working late was normal and expected in her firm. In particular, Emma wanted her written work to be flawless. She prided herself on her perfect grammar and formatting, spending hours tidying up her documents and making sure every period was in the right place. While the perfection in Emma's reports largely went unnoticed by the partners, her growing exhaustion was much more obvious. Emma often worked more than twelve hours a day, only to return home and collapse into bed. After hitting the gym early in the morning, she'd head in to repeat the cycle again. Emma had little time to see friends and on weekends spent most of her time catching up on sleep. She felt drained, but kept going because she did not want to disappoint her managers.

Do you work too hard? Briefly describe a situation where you work excessively hard and don't get much better results from your effort.

_____

_____

_____

_____

_____

Taking on Too Much

When your standards are incredibly high, and you simply must do *everything* to this standard *all the time,* you can end up incredibly busy trying to reach this standard. You may have difficulty telling the difference between tasks that are urgent and important and tasks that just don't need the same effort. If you treat a small, unimportant follow-up email with the same importance as a major report to the board, you'll have a to-do list that you can never finish and feel under extraordinary pressure. If you try to keep everyone happy all the time too, it can feel impossible to let any of it go.

Simona was frantically busy all the time. During the day, she was completing her honors year in environmental science. She'd spent a year collecting data, interviewing stakeholders around the state, collecting soil and water samples, and doing complex statistical analysis of her results. Simona's supervisors had told her that the project was big enough to be an entire PhD. She already had a job lined up next year, but remained determined to get the top grade for her work. In addition to her thesis, Simona was still seeing friends, going to the gym, coordinating two clubs on campus, working one night a week, seeing her family, and doing the final coursework for her degree. Simona treated every assignment as equally important despite many of them being worth little to her final grade. She treated every task as essential and could not see how she could drop anything. Feeling a sense of impending doom, Simona became irritable and teary when she thought about how much work she'd need to complete by the end of the semester.

Do you take on too much? Describe several situations where you push yourself too hard and feel unable to compromise on achieving your standards.

_____

_____

_____

_____

_____

Avoiding Feedback

Feedback can be terrifying. Any feedback, even the constructive kind, infers that you are not perfect, and that can be confronting. You might hear that you've done a decent job and want to know people are happy with your work, but you never know what feedback you'll get until *after* they've said it. This uncertainty is so uncomfortable. And, even if you get 99 percent positive feedback and one suggestion for improvement, I can guess what you'll focus on. It can seem easier to avoid feedback altogether.

In my thirties, I ran a company with my husband where we delivered coaching and leadership programs. As part of my professional development, I had the chance to get performance feedback using 360-degree feedback. This is where your peers, other managers, and staff complete a questionnaire about your leadership. This was very scary for me, even though I had good relationships with the team. When the survey was done, I felt extremely anxious about the results and postponed the feedback to a later date. No one pushed me to do it, and I kept putting it off for months. Even today, I still feel embarrassed to tell you that I never got that feedback.

Do you dread feedback and avoid it if possible? Describe a situation when you avoid feedback or when receiving feedback causes you distress and anxiety.

_____

_____

_____

_____

_____

Seeking Reassurance

Reassurance from others can help alleviate your feelings of doubt, insecurity, and the nagging worry that you've made a mistake. Seeking reassurance is a way of getting rid of your feelings of uncertainty and insecurity, but it rarely feels completely satisfying. While at first you might feel relieved, this feeling often doesn't last for long. Repeatedly asking for reassurance can put a strain on your relationships and people may see you as insecure or needy.

Kiara worked as an administrative assistant in a busy financial planning office. She knew that when she was reporting on people's finances, it was important to be exact. Kiara aimed to do her job flawlessly and was always worried about whether her manager was pleased with her. Kiara wanted to feel certain everything was fine, so several times a day, she would check if her manager was happy with what she'd done. Privately, Kiara's manager was concerned about her lack of confidence, and when it was time to appoint someone as office coordinator, she named a newer member of the team instead. Kiara was devastated that her exceptional performance had been overlooked, the decision only confirming her fears that her manager was not happy with her.

Do you seek reassurance? Briefly describe a situation where you've sought reassurance in a way that was unhelpful.

_____

_____

_____

_____

_____

Struggling to Make Decisions

Decisions are difficult to make when you must always get things right. Even if you spend a lot of time analyzing your decision, researching, and seeking advice, you can continue to feel unsure. Decisions big and small can be difficult. Big decisions such as whether to apply for a new job or which college program to study are often challenging. You know that even the most detailed job description won't tell you whether you'll enjoy the work, and no college degree will automatically lead you to a job that suits you. Even small decisions such as what to wear out for dinner or whether to date someone new can be worrisome as there is no guarantee that your decision will be correct. After all, what if you don't like the food or the date doesn't work out well? Trying to be certain is what keeps you stuck, and if you can't decide at all, you might miss out completely.

Jasmin was just out of school and didn't know what to do next. For several years, she had been thinking about becoming a social worker or youth counselor. She remembered the tough time she had as a young child and wanted to help other children who were experiencing family breakdown and conflict. Jasmin looked at courses online, and while she made some inquiries about the timetable and the cost, she didn't enroll. Worrying that she wouldn't be able to do the study or get a job in the area, Jasmin thought, "What if I waste my time?," "What if I don't like it?," and "What if I can't do the work?" Jasmin got a summer job in her local hardware store to save up some money for college, but when fall arrived, she stayed, telling her colleagues she needed to earn more money. Jasmin felt stuck, too scared of making a mistake to take the next step.

Do you struggle to make decisions? Briefly describe a situation where you've found it difficult to make a choice and it has caused you problems.

_____

_____

_____

_____

_____

Playing It Safe and Avoiding Things Completely

Do you tend to say no to new opportunities because you are nervous or uneasy? Maybe this has even become your default answer whenever someone asks you to try something new. If you can never make a mistake, it is difficult to take risks. You may not even realize you are in a habit of taking the safest option. You might find good reasons not to ask for a raise, apply for a supervisor role, or ask for new challenges at work. You might stay single because dating feels so terribly risky and vulnerable. But by playing it safe, you avoid the feelings of fear, doubt, and uncertainty that come with the possibility of failure. Yet, all great opportunities come with some element of risk, and if you want to achieve things without ever making a mistake, you'll never be able to do anything new. By staying in your lane and keeping things as they are, exciting opportunities can pass you by. In the end, life becomes smaller and duller.

When I was a child, I avoided team sports as much as I could. I didn't want to do something I wasn't good at. Whenever I played a team sport at school, I worried about missing a shot and letting the team down. I would blame myself if the team lost. Of course, because I rarely played sports, I never became any better at them either. They became even easier to avoid in my adult life and I found other ways to keep fit. I know I missed a lot of fun in my childhood because, in recent years, I have been doing outdoor group fitness classes and we often play ballgames between other activities. These are non-competitive games among friends—so of course, we all try extremely hard to win! At first, I had my old worries that I would drop the ball or make a bad pass. Yet, over time, I've improved my ball skills and these games have become one of my favorite parts of the workout.

Do you play it safe and say no to new opportunities? Briefly describe a situation where you've missed out on something great as a result.

_____

_____

_____

_____

_____

All unhelpful perfectionistic patterns can get in the way of living a life that matters. They shrink what is possible and make life less rewarding. In this next table, you can evaluate which of these patterns cause the biggest problems for you.

Self-Evaluation: Identifying Your Most Unhelpful Habits

Circle a number to indicate how much of a problem this behavior pattern is for you.

Unhelpful Pattern	Not a Problem at All								Large Problem, Interferes with My Life
Procrastination	1	2	3	4	5	6	7	8	9	10
Excessive Checking	1	2	3	4	5	6	7	8	9	10
Working Too Hard	1	2	3	4	5	6	7	8	9	10
Taking on Too Much	1	2	3	4	5	6	7	8	9	10
Avoiding Feedback	1	2	3	4	5	6	7	8	9	10
Seeking Reassurance	1	2	3	4	5	6	7	8	9	10
Struggling to Make Decisions	1	2	3	4	5	6	7	8	9	10
Playing It Safe	1	2	3	4	5	6	7	8	9	10
Avoiding Things Completely	1	2	3	4	5	6	7	8	9	10

As you look over your results, you will find some areas are more problematic than others. Which three patterns cause the biggest problems for you? Write these down.

1. _____

2. _____

3. _____

At this point, it would be easy to feel frustrated at yourself for the unhelpful things you've been doing, the problems this has caused you, and the opportunities you've missed. You might feel disappointed that you've been continuing to do these things, even though they've caused you so much pain. You might want to fix this straightaway. Can you offer yourself this little kindness and understanding in this moment? Can you start where you are?

Start Where You Are

Do you ever want to be better at something right away? I know I do. I'd prefer to step straight into a future where I have mastered a new skill than struggle with learning something from scratch. I don't enjoy starting out being bad at something. Since I want to do well at *everything,* it can be hard to be a beginner again because of the high chance I'll make a mistake.

It helps to remember that any time you want to learn something new, you can only start from where you are. There are no quick fixes to long-standing behavior patterns. The path to successful change requires knowing exactly what you want to change—and consistent effort to make that change. Defining your goals can be your first step toward change, but *how* you set these goals can set you up for failure. Perfectionists often set goals in ways that make them impossible to achieve. So, in this next section, you'll set yourself up for positive change in a new way. You'll also work out what you really need to change, and how to approach change to maximize your chance of success.

Letting Go of Perfect Goals

The first trap perfectionists fall into is setting "perfect forever goals." I uncover these goals in my work with clients every day: goals that are too big, too challenging, and demand perfection. Unspoken within these goals is an expectation that your change will continue *forever* without any bad days, slip-ups, or distractions. Any goal set like this is exceedingly difficult to achieve because it works more like a perfectionistic rule.

One common example of a perfect forever goal is going on a strict diet. Successfully changing your eating habits requires that you change how you behave *in the long term.* Unfortunately, most people don't approach going on a diet in this way. If you've ever been on a crash diet, you may remember the first day you start. You say something like, "I will eat only these certain foods and stop any snacking on sugary treats, starting right now." Implied is that you will *never* eat the wrong foods *ever again*. The problem with this goal is that it demands exceptional performance and makes no allowance for mistakes or the ability to have cake on your birthday. You have failed the first time you have a cookie or chocolate, and you might feel so frustrated and demoralized, you decide to finish the whole packet.

Goals that require perfection and last forever are ineffective when it comes to changing behavior because after any slip-up, you've automatically failed, and each time this happens, it becomes harder to start again. Over time, you develop something called "learned helplessness": you give up trying because you feel like there is no way you can succeed (Lee-Baggley 2019).

Briefly describe an unsuccessful perfect forever goal that you've set in the past:

_____

_____

_____

_____

Describe what happened when you failed to achieve this goal:

_____

_____

_____

_____

There is an alternative method of setting goals that is much more successful. You focus on small, specific changes, practice these until they become comfortable and consistent habits, and only then do you change something else. You keep doing this, gradually, over time. To change your diet, you might start by decreasing the frequency of days when you drink soda and increasing the frequency of days where you eat a healthy lunch. Wherever you start, you then build from there. When the first new habit is becoming well-established, you add more positive changes such as reducing your sugary treats after dinner and going for a walk instead. If you keep track of how often you achieve the new behaviors and keep working on them, over time, you'll notice your new habits developing. Building on a foundation of small reliable successes is more effective than changing a lot of things at once and not being consistent with any of them (Leonard-Curtin and Leonard-Curtin 2019). Doing more of what works will be both encouraging and motivating.

Setting Goals That Work for You

While initially you might focus on the kinds of things you don't want to feel or do anymore, such as "not being so hard on myself," "not feeling so depressed," "not worrying about things," or "not working so hard," unfortunately, goals like this aren't helpful. In ACT, goals that focus on things you *don't want* are called "dead person's goals" because they are things that a dead body could do better than you. In general, such goals aren't something worth aiming toward. A dead person, for example, is always going to be better than you at not losing their temper, but they are not going to be good at being kind, patient, and loving. Goals that tell you what to do—rather than what *not* to do—give you something to aim toward, whereas goals that focus on getting rid of experiences or stopping certain behaviors are hard to put into action because they *don't tell you what you need to do.* It is harder to work toward the absence of something, so these goals tend to leave you stuck. Choose goals that move you toward the things that matter.

Other common but ineffective goals focus on feeling better. These are called "emotional goals." Wanting to feel good is understandable, particularly if you've been struggling with having a low mood or anxiety for a while. Good feelings come and go according to what we do, and also depend on what happens around us. You can only guarantee "feeling happy" or "being positive" if you control your emotions and the entire world around you. You can avoid people and places that make you feel sad or anxious, but eventually, this will have consequences and make your life small and depressing. Back in Chapter 3, you saw how little lasting control you have over your inner experiences. This is why goals that are designed to ensure positive emotions are destined to fail.

Goals that focus on practical steps you can take to make things better are much more helpful. When these actions align with your values, you'll feel good about doing them. These are called "valued goals," and they describe how to move toward a life that is meaningful for you. When you do this in incremental changes, you are more likely to make progress, and change becomes deceptively simple: do the things that move you in the direction of your values and add to this over time.

Activity: The Difference Between Dead Person's Goals,
Emotional Goals, and Valued Goals

Read each of the following statements and select whether each statement is a dead person's goal, an emotional goal, or a valued goal.

Goal Statement	Dead Person's Goal	Emotional Goal	Valued Goal
1. Don't yell at my children			
2. Have higher self-esteem			
3. Be more patient with my children			
4. Be happier			
5. Stop being so hard on myself			
6. Express myself creatively through art			
7. Stop worrying so much			
8. Think positively			
9. Stop feeling so depressed			
10. Be a caring friend			
11. Help in my local community			
12. Don't think so negatively			
13. Don't be so hard on myself			
14. Be compassionate toward myself			
15. Get rid of painful memories			
16. Feel good about myself			
17. Deliver high-quality work			
18. Be thin			
19. Be more relaxed			
20. Learn how to speak a new language			

Answers to the questions above:

Dead Person's Goals: 1, 5, 7, 9, 12, 13, 15, 18

Emotional Goals: 2, 4, 8, 16, 19

Valued Goals: 3, 6, 10, 11, 14, 17, 20

Let's look at what valued goals would look like in practice for Xavier, who was procrastinating on his thesis.

Xavier knew his procrastination was a problem and told himself that he had to "stop procrastinating" right away and "get on with the work." Unfortunately, he didn't know how to simply stop this pattern. If he could, he would have done so already. So, Xavier focused on what he needed to do and then broke the problem down into tangible actions to help him achieve this.

Xavier's Perfectionistic Goal: *Stop procrastinating*

Xavier's Valued Goal: *Improve my ability to focus on my work and get back on track when I get distracted or feel overwhelmed.*

Action Steps:

- "Break the work down into small chunks and create a list of things to do that I can check off when complete."

- "Before I start working, use Soothing Rhythm Breathing and acknowledge how I'm feeling."

- "Remind myself why doing this is important (review my values)."

- "Acknowledge how difficult it is to focus for a long time and schedule myself short breaks every thirty minutes."

- "Expect to get distracted, and when this happens, notice what I'm feeling and the sensations in my body, take a deep breath, and then return to my work."

Rather than attempt to achieve all these changes at once, Xavier gradually added these changes over time, making them yet more achievable. Xavier's change wasn't perfect. He still found himself distracted quite often, but over time, he got better at returning to his work and began making real progress toward completing his thesis.

Xavier's valued goal focused on what he needed to do and included steps that helped him both manage his emotions and build his ability to focus. There were two skills Xavier really needed to achieve his goal: the ability to *notice* whenever he got distracted and then the ability to get himself back on track. Strengthening these skills made long-term change more possible.

Living a Lifetime of Gentle Returns

To change your perfectionism into something that works better, you will need to try new things. Along the way, you will stumble, mess up, get off track and lose your way. You'll probably have to start over more than once. All change is an imperfect process. Change feels weird, confusing, and unsettling. Yet, allowing yourself to feel uncomfortable and risk failing is the only way you can make progress. "Bad days," "missteps," and "mistakes" are a natural and expected part of any change, and although this does not fit well with a perfectionistic approach, to make lasting change, you will need to accept this. Your fear of failing and the uncomfortable feelings that come with this are likely to show up each time you attempt to change.

Think about a time when you have drifted away from doing what's important and briefly describe it below.

_____

_____

_____

Now describe a time when you've gotten back on track, what was involved, and how you felt doing this.

_____

_____

_____

Professor Kelly Wilson, one of the founders of ACT, beautifully describes our tendency to drift away from what's important across our lives, and how we need to keep getting back on track as living "a lifetime of gentle returns" (Wilson and Murrell 2004). Changing your unhelpful perfectionism into more helpful habits will challenge you to learn *that your failures are not final* and that *you can recover from your mistakes.* Can you make room for the discomfort of being a novice? Can you recover from your disappointment when you find you've fallen back into old habits? Can you continue to *start where you are?*

Taking Steps Toward Your Values

Now that you've explored how to set goals, in the last section of this chapter you will identify what it is you want to change by defining three valued goals and coming up with some small steps that would help you achieve each goal and move you closer to what matters in your life.

Activity: Setting Valued Goals

Start this activity by noting down no more than three perfectionistic habits you want to change. Choose from the unhelpful habits that cause the biggest problems in your life. You might like to look back through your answers to the checklists and activities in this book for inspiration.

1. _____

   _____

2. _____

   _____

3. _____

   _____

Now using the following worksheet, break down each problem area in detail, describing:

1. the unhelpful behaviors you want to change

2. what valued action you'd like to be doing instead (your valued goal)

3. your values relevant to this area of your life

4. the fear that is driving your unhelpful habit (Big Bad)

5. the uncomfortable inner experiences that come with your Big Bad

6. what steps you could take to change this habit and move toward your values

As you complete each one, make sure your valued goals:

- target an area that is causing you a lot of problems (the 10 percent)

- are not over-ambitious and don't require perfection to be successful

- are easy enough that you can experience some success right away

- really matter to you

- consider the impact of uncomfortable emotions, thoughts, and sensations that are likely to emerge

- allow for errors, lapses, and continual improvement.

Use the worksheets provided in this book or download a copy from http://www.newharbinger .com/48077.

Worksheet: Setting Valued Goals (Example 1)

My Unhelpful Habit: What I want to stop doing.	I get frustrated with my kids when they misbehave, and I lose my temper and shout at them.
Valued Goal:	Be more patient with my kids.
My Values:	Being a calm, warm, kind, and patient mom.
My Fear of Failure (Big Bad):	People will judge me.
Unwanted Inner Experiences: Uncomfortable experiences that come with my Big Bad.	My body feels tense and under pressure. I feel like I'm a kettle going to boil over.
My Valued Actions: Steps I will take toward my values.	• Take a deep breath and calm myself down. • If I can't speak with a warm, calm tone, take a pause before speaking or tell my child we'll talk about this later. • Remember that their behavior is not a reflection of me as a person. • Think about what might be upsetting my child and what their emotional needs might be at that time. • Only talk to my child when I am calm.

Worksheet: Setting Valued Goals (Example 2)

My Unhelpful Habit: What I want to stop doing.	I am slow at finishing my work because I spend too long checking it.
Valued Goal:	I do my work efficiently and hand things in on time by checking things once or twice only.
My Values:	I am a good team member, delivering high-quality work on time to support the team.
My Fear of Failure (Big Bad):	I don't want my manager to think I'm incompetent.
Unwanted Inner Experiences: Uncomfortable experiences that come with my Big Bad.	I feel sick in my stomach if I think I've made a mistake.
My Valued Actions: Steps I will take toward my values.	• Gently remind myself that it's important to me to support the team and get my work done. • Practice my Soothing Rhythm Breathing if I get anxious. • Pay attention when I'm reading things the first time, so I don't have to read them again. • Practice reducing my checking behavior, starting with only checking my emails twice before sending. • Once I am doing okay with this, limit myself to doing two edits before handing in reports. • Avoid rereading emails after I've sent them to reassure myself.

Worksheet: My Valued Goal #1

My Unhelpful Habit: What I want to stop doing.	
Valued Goal:	
My Values:	
My Fear of Failure (Big Bad):	
Unwanted Inner Experiences: Uncomfortable experiences that come with my Big Bad.	
My Valued Actions: Steps I will take toward my values.	• • • • • • •

Worksheet: My Valued Goal #2

My Unhelpful Habit: What I want to stop doing.	
Valued Goal:	
My Values:	
My Fear of Failure (Big Bad):	
Unwanted Inner Experiences: Uncomfortable experiences that come with my Big Bad.	
My Valued Actions: Steps I will take toward my values.	• • • • • • •

Worksheet: My Valued Goal #3

My Unhelpful Habit: What I want to stop doing.	
Valued Goal:	
My Values:	
My Fear of Failure (Big Bad):	
Unwanted Inner Experiences: Uncomfortable experiences that come with my Big Bad.	
My Valued Actions: Steps I will take toward my values.	• • • • • • •

Putting It Together

Procrastination, working too hard, taking on too much, checking things too many times, avoiding feedback, seeking reassurance, struggling to make decisions, and avoiding situations where you might fail are common problems for people who struggle with unhelpful perfectionism. Some of these are likely to be problems for you too. Even though it can seem like these problems are insurmountable, you do not need to change everything to make a substantial difference in your life. There are likely to be a small number of habits that cause most of your problems, and this chapter has been about discovering what these are.

By targeting the key behaviors that cause you the most problems (the most troublesome 10 percent), you can transform your perfectionism into something that works better for you. After all, most of the perfectionistic things you do can be helpful at times, and if you can be flexible and adjust your behavior according to the situation, these habits can help make your life better.

There are no quick fixes to perfectionism and trying to change your perfectionism *perfectly* won't work. Successful change is not a single decision, but rather *a lifetime of gentle returns,* where you cycle back repeatedly to what matters. Successfully changing your behavior will require persistent effort. It will push you to cope with getting things wrong along the way. Whenever you are making change, your fear of failure will show up through uncomfortable thoughts, feelings, and sensations, and you'll need to accommodate these experiences too.

In this chapter, you've had an opportunity to think about how you'd like to behave in areas that are causing you problems, and at the end of this chapter, you've set some goals for change. These probably look quite different from goals you've set before. Instead of setting goals that are large, ambitious, push you toward excellence, chase positive feelings, or take you away from the uncomfortable situations, I've asked you to set goals that are small, practical, and aligned with your values. It's goals like these that will set you up for success.

Taking Small Imperfect Steps: Your Personal Action Plan

Before you move on, take this opportunity to develop your Personal Action Plan.

What did you learn in this chapter that was relevant to you?

1. _____

2. _____

3. _____

What did you learn about yourself?

1. _____

2. _____

3. _____

Over the coming days, what small actions would you be willing to take toward a life where your perfectionism is more helpful for you?

1. _____

2. _____

3. _____

CHAPTER 6

Learning to Be Kinder to Yourself

A moment of self-compassion can change your entire day. A string of such moments can change the course of your life.

—Christopher K. Germer

At some point, you stopped being kind to yourself. Instead, you became a harsh critic of yourself as a person, and of the things you do. Being hard on yourself is one of the core processes of unhelpful perfectionism because it is woven into every problem it causes. When you approach yourself as the enemy, the implications are enormous for your mental health, well-being, and ability to reach your goals. Criticizing yourself when you don't meet your own exacting (and ever-higher) standards will leave you feeling anxious, stressed, and demoralized. You can intensely fear the criticism that comes with making a mistake. Knowing you will feel terrible if you fail can make you reluctant to start anything new. For this reason, learning to be kinder to yourself is an essential part of transforming your unhelpful perfectionism into habits that will lead you toward a life you love.

From his teens until his late twenties, Dalian had lived a fit and healthy lifestyle, working as a personal trainer and competing in endurance events and marathons. He'd worked hard in training, pushed his body to the limits, and kept a strict diet to improve his performance. Now in his early forties, Dalian had a chaotic and often unhealthy lifestyle. He'd put on some weight and rarely cooked, instead eating junk food and takeout most days. He drank half a bottle of wine most weeknights and more on weekends. When Dalian unexpectedly developed a serious heart condition called atrial fibrillation, he was shocked and uneasy. Periodically and without warning, Dalian's heart would beat irregularly, and he'd feel dizzy, weak, and extremely tired. He was in and out of the hospital and put on a waiting list for surgery, without which he had a higher risk of blood clots, stroke, and heart failure.

Dalian's doctors told him that to have the best chance of a full recovery he needed to improve his diet, stop drinking alcohol, exercise regularly, and take regular medication. Dalian could see the importance of this, but he struggled to eat healthily for more than a few days, quickly getting tempted by sugary snacks, junk food, and wine. He remembered how perfectly he'd managed his eating in the past and felt furious at himself for his failure to make the changes he needed. Dalian's mind swirled with thoughts like, "I am so hopeless," "I should be able to do this," and "This should be easy—what's wrong with me?" Dalian felt completely defeated and, in the end, it just seemed too hard to make any changes at all.

Dalian's self-criticism undermined his ability to put these quite difficult changes in place. Being hard on himself got in the way of things that were crucial, like his health. Self-criticism can affect many aspects of your life in this way. Read the following list and place a checkmark next to any that apply to you.

I tend to be angry, upset, and critical of myself when I:

☐ Make a mistake

☐ Don't meet my standards

☐ Procrastinate on important work

☐ Feel scared of new challenges

☐ Avoid social events

☐ Think about my body shape, size, or appearance

☐ Don't maintain a healthy diet and exercise routine

☐ Don't feel motivated to do new things

☐ Struggle with anxiety, depression, or other aspects of my mental health

☐ Get stuck in patterns of behavior I know aren't helpful for me

☐ Feel afraid of being judged by others

Describe several situations where you tend to get angry, frustrated, critical, or disappointed with yourself below.

_____

_____

_____

_____

If you checked several of the items on the list above, then you will be familiar with feelings of self-doubt and defeat. There are many changes you can make to your unhelpful perfectionistic behaviors, but learning to be kinder to yourself is likely to create the biggest positive change in how you feel _and_ what you achieve in life. Changing your attitude toward yourself will also improve your mental health by alleviating feelings of stress, anxiety, and pressure, and can help improve your relationships with others.

Are You Willing to Be Kinder to Yourself?

It is one thing for me to tell you to be kinder to yourself, but it may be a challenge for you to do it. It may even seem like an impossible task. Even though being hard on yourself has caused you a lot of pain, it might be difficult to let it go. Many people believe that they must be tough on themselves and feel reluctant to change this. Take a moment to explore your own beliefs. Listed below are some of the common justifications that people offer for the way they criticize themselves. Check any statements with which you agree.

- ☐ I need to be self-critical to motivate myself. Without this, I will be lazy and unproductive.

- ☐ If I don't criticize myself, I will just make the same mistakes again.

- ☐ I need to criticize myself to improve my performance.

- ☐ Being kind to myself would make me too weak, soft, or vulnerable to being hurt.

- ☐ I don't deserve to be kind to myself. Other people deserve kindness more than me.

- ☐ It would be selfish and indulgent to be kind to myself.

- ☐ If I am kind to myself, I will become an arrogant or self-centered person and people won't like me.

☐   Being kind to yourself is not realistic. I should recognize and point out my mistakes so I can improve.

☐   It's easier to keep doing what I've been doing.

☐   I don't know how to be kind to myself.

If you checked a few of these boxes, you might feel quite wedded to the need to be tough on yourself. Even if you might think it's necessary, consider whether doing this is so helpful for you overall. We all make mistakes and it's important to learn from them and fix things where you can. When you've hurt someone, it's important to apologize and make amends. However, does it help you to criticize yourself for your mistakes while you do this? Does criticizing yourself really prevent mistakes from ever happening again?

Over this chapter and the next, you will find a series of activities that will help you learn to be kinder to yourself *while still holding yourself accountable for achieving your goals*. Collectively, the skills you will learn are known as "self-compassion." In this next section, we will explore the foundations of self-compassion and why it is such an important skill to learn.

The Origin and Purpose of Self-Compassion

Self-compassion has been part of human behavior since our early ancestors were living a nomadic life in the jungle, savannah, and forests. These early humans developed three physiological systems that allowed them to respond effectively to the world around them by protecting them from threats (a "threat and self-protection system"), motivating them to find the resources they need (a "drive and resource-seeking system"), and helping them to rest, recover and find safeness with each other (a "contentment and soothing system") (Gilbert 2009, Kolts 2016). These emotion regulation systems, together with our ancestors' ability to use language and solve complex problems, can explain why humans have been so successful in populating the world.

We have the same brain structure as our ancestors. The way you respond to threats, seek resources, and soothe yourself uses these same emotion regulation systems, even though you live in a vastly different physical and social environment. In today's world, these ancient emotion regulation systems respond to different threats and desires, and if you don't pay attention, they can lead you down some unhelpful pathways. The way you respond to rigid perfectionistic standards and fear of failure is one of these situations.

Detecting and Managing Threats

Our ancestors developed a finely tuned system to protect them from dangers such as predators, deadly animals, and natural disasters. Having a rapid response threat and self-protection system was essential in helping our ancestors identify threats and prepare to respond by running, fighting, or hiding. Prioritizing threats over all other experiences helped your ancestors to survive and produce children, so you are the result of that system working well.

Today's threats are quite different. When you see failures such as making a mistake or being socially rejected as dangerous to your well-being, the threat system responds by triggering the same running, fighting, or hiding response, only now it looks like procrastination, checking, reassurance-seeking, or avoiding the things you fear. You do these things to help you escape the potential loss, embarrassment, or hurt of a mistake. When you criticize yourself for the mistake, this only makes things worse. The criticism triggers your threat system further, making you even more fearful and vigilant. No wonder you can end up chronically anxious and on edge.

> *Christie worried constantly that her friends didn't like her. She was scared that she wasn't good enough to be their friend and was sure they'd somehow find this out. Christie wanted them to like her, so she tried to be the most thoughtful friend possible. She worked hard to be funny, friendly, and considerate of their needs. She bought them presents on their birthdays (as well as on Valentine's Day, Easter, and Christmas) even though no one else bought presents. If someone was upset because they'd broken up with their boyfriend or got a bad grade, Christie would send them messages and memes to cheer them up. Her friends knew that this was just "Christie being Christie," but sometimes they still found this attention a little too much. Quietly, they grumbled to each other that Christie could be a "bit too intense" and "tried too hard."*

Christie's fear of losing her friends has put her threat system on high alert, and over time, her threat system has become chronically overactive. Christie feels compelled to make sure her friends like her, and to reduce her anxiety, she does all sorts of things to try to make this happen. Unfortunately, these habits create bigger problems because they move Christie even closer to what she most fears: losing her friends.

Consider whether your threat system might be trying to protect you from failure and rejection. Which of the following best describes your threat system? (Circle one.)

Not sufficiently active	Appropriately active	Mix of under and overactive	Sometimes overactive	Very often overactive

Briefly describe situations where your threat system gets overactive.

_____

_____

_____

_____

_____

Finding Resources to Survive and Prosper

Beyond protecting themselves from threats, to survive, our ancestors needed to find the resources required to flourish as a community such as food, water, shelter, social connections, sexual partners, and status in the community or tribe. The drive and resource-seeking system motivated and energized our ancestors to seek out these things by stimulating feelings of excitement, desire, and ambition (Kolts 2016). Achieving success triggered the dopamine reward centers of the brain, creating positive feelings that motivated our ancestors to keep striving.

In the modern world, our goals have changed; our measures of success now including high grades, material possessions, a successful career, and social status. Seeking the rewards and stimulation that comes from success can become all-encompassing. Measuring your success against your ambitious standards can push you to keep striving beyond what you really need, without regard for the costs. If your drive system becomes chronically overactive, you can end up working too hard, taking on too much, and getting overwhelmed.

Now in her final year of high school, Tala had pushed herself hard for as long as she could remember. Tala hoped to go to college, but she needed a scholarship to get there because her parents could not afford the tuition fees. As the child of immigrants who'd struggled to make ends meet, Tala felt like she owed it to her parents to do well and not waste the opportunity they'd given her. She worked hard in class and did her best to get good grades for every paper. She also played trumpet in three ensembles, played tennis twice a week, was on the school debate team, and had a part-time job. Tala felt like she couldn't afford to slack off or make any mistakes; she must keep up the pressure on herself or else she would fail.

Determined to succeed, Tala increasingly structured her life around study. When preparing for exams, Tala reviewed her notes daily and did as many practice papers as she could find. Sticking to a strict daily routine, Tala would study late into the night, then drag herself from bed each morning to start over. Even though she felt tired in her body, Tala's mind was racing, and she was filled with nervous energy. However, with her anxiety and exhaustion rising, Tala found it increasingly difficult to concentrate and despite her efforts, her grades started slipping.

Tala's threat and drive systems are both in overdrive. Her fear of failing (the threat) and desire to succeed push her to work ever harder, yet in the end, she risks losing what she is striving for.

Briefly describe any situations where your drive system gets overactive, and you work too hard, end up overwhelmed and exhausted.

_____

_____

_____

_____

_____

While many people slip into a pattern of working too hard, some respond the opposite way—they stop trying because they realize that they can never meet their own standards or completely avoid failure. They avoid risks by playing it safe and pulling away from uncomfortable situations altogether.

Sean worked hard at school and gained a scholarship for college. Now entering his final year, Sean knew he needed a perfect GPA to get into the engineering program he wanted, and he was on track to get it. Yet, on top of managing a hectic study load, Sean also had to manage a chronic illness. Sean had been diagnosed with Type I diabetes when he was eight years old after he noticed blurred vision when playing sports. Sean's parents looked after him well during his childhood and early teens, but in his final years of school, Sean took control of his treatment. Like many people, the daily demands of checking his blood sugar and adjusting his insulin frustrated and bored Sean. He understood what was needed, but also knew he could never get it completely right. Sean felt demoralized and defeated, and in response, he ignored the problem. Instead of doing the calculations, he'd guess what insulin he needed, leaving his blood sugar to get too high. Instead of looking after his health, Sean pushed hard in his studies, where he was enjoying doing well.

Sean wanted to do everything in his life to the highest standard, but because he couldn't manage his diabetes that way, he got frustrated. While Sean's drive system was activated to achieve his study goals, it became the opposite for his health—he gave up.

Briefly describe situations where your drive system becomes underactive, and you've wanted to give up or get away.

_____

_____

_____

_____

Consider your drive system and how it might be pushing you to be your best. Which of the following best describes your drive system? (Circle one.)

Not sufficiently active	Appropriately active	Mix of under and overactive	Sometimes overactive	Very often overactive

Feeling Content and Safe

When there were no threats to defend themselves from and they had the resources they needed, the contentment and soothing system helped our ancestors to feel safe, peaceful, and content (Kolts 2016). This system allowed the body to rest, recover, digest food, heal from injury, and lower unhealthy stress levels. It also helped our ancestors to build their communities and strengthen their connections with each other.

Modern life holds different stressors to those faced by our ancestors. We live in an environment filled with nutritionally inadequate food, sedentary jobs, work stress, and complex family systems, and this makes our life complicated and unhealthy. Add to this living with the threat of failure, the pain of self-criticism, and rigid personal standards you cannot reach, and you can see why so many people feel chronically unsafe, uncertain, and disconnected from others. If you do not have the ability to calm and soothe yourself, you will always be vulnerable to boredom, loneliness, disconnection, anxiety, and anger.

Consider how your soothing system might help you recover, connect, and heal. Which of the following best describes your soothing system? (Circle one.)

Not sufficiently active	Appropriately active	Mix of under and overactive	Sometimes overactive	Very often overactive

Briefly describe situations where your soothing system gets most activated:

_____

_____

_____

_____

_____

The emotion regulation systems work best when they are balanced with each other. When you struggle with unhelpful perfectionism, the threat system can become chronically overactive and the drive systems can swing between being underactive or overactive. Often the soothing system is chronically underactive. You can balance these systems by activating your soothing system using self-compassion. You can learn how to calm yourself and find new, kinder ways of relating to your struggle. When the soothing system is balanced with the threat and drive systems, you are able to feel motivated, prepared, alert, energized, and safe *at the same time*. Developing the skills of self-compassion can help you achieve this.

Self-compassion is not about finding bliss, dropping out, or hiding from threats. Developing compassion for yourself will build feelings of satisfaction and contentment. It can help motivate you to move toward what you value, and face your fears with courage *and* compassion. You can learn to encourage yourself to do better and be kinder to yourself when you falter. Developing the skills needed to be compassionate toward yourself is what you will focus on for the rest of this chapter and the next.

I encourage you to explore self-compassion beyond the exercises in this book. Self-compassion is a rapidly growing area of psychological research and practice, and there are many interesting books and websites available. Check out Kristin Neff's site, Selfcompassion.org, where you can assess your current capacity for self-compassion and identify areas where you can improve. Seek out books by authors such as Paul Gilbert, Laura Silberstein-Tirch, Dennis Tirch, and Russell Kolts, who have all written some lovely and practical guides to self-compassion.

What Is Self-Compassion?

Compassion might be easy to offer to other people, but it can be a completely different story when it comes to offering compassion to yourself. Self-compassion is a skill that can be hard to learn because you must first pay attention to your own suffering. Noticing how you are feeling can be uncomfortable because these are thoughts, emotions, and physical sensations that you would rather not have. Yet, throughout this book, you've been building your ability to tolerate inner discomfort in small ways. Each time I've asked you to pay attention to your uncomfortable thoughts, emotions, and inner sensations, you've been practicing this skill.

Building on this foundation, you can add the other elements of self-compassion: having a warm, kind, and gentle approach to yourself and your suffering; being sensitive to your own distress; not judging yourself for struggling; and being motivated to help. In the next activity, you'll explore what this looks like using a story called "The Two Teachers" (Gilbert 2009, Kolts 2016). Each teacher reflects a different way of treating yourself, one of which contains all the elements of self-compassion.

Activity: The Two Teachers

Imagine you are the parent of a small child who is just starting school. Your child is a normally developing five-year-old, and as such, they find learning to read and write challenging. They are also not used to sitting down for extended periods and can get restless and distracted.

Now imagine your child has two teachers (job share arrangements are common in schools nowadays, after all). The first teacher focuses on everything your child is doing wrong. They constantly point out your child's mistakes and get irritated easily. This teacher tries to make your child feel bad about what they are doing, and using a cold and harsh tone of voice, they say things to your child like:

"The other children are sitting down nicely. Why can't you?"

"You need to try harder."

"Why aren't you focusing on your work?"

"You should be doing better at this by now."

"The other kids understand this—what's wrong with you?"

(How awful. It makes me shudder to think of my child having a teacher like this.)

The second teacher is completely different. This teacher is warm and understanding. They look for the strengths in your child and find opportunities for them to use these skills in class. They celebrate your child's successes and encourage them to take pride in their work. In class, they pull up a chair next to your child and while looking kindly into their eyes, they say things like:

"I see that you are struggling with this—let's work out what help you need."

"I like what you've done here—can you do more of that?"

"How about we go over this again?"

"Let's do a bit more of this together before you go out to play."

Which teacher would you like for your child? (Circle one.)

        The first teacher   The second teacher

Which teacher is most likely to help your child learn, grow, and build their confidence? (Circle one.)

        The first teacher   The second teacher

Describe the personal qualities this teacher has that would most help your child.

_____

_____

_____

Which teacher is most like the way you talk to yourself? (Circle one.)

        The first teacher   The second teacher

Describe the personal qualities this teacher has that would undermine your learning, growth, and self-confidence.

_____

_____

_____

"The Two Teachers" story illustrates how the way you treat yourself can influence not only your sense of well-being but also your ability to learn and grow. The personal qualities showed by the second teacher including being:

1. Warm, gentle, and kind

2. Empathetic and understanding

3. Accepting and not judgmental

4. Motivated to help

5. Encouraging and supportive while still holding your child accountable to complete the work ("Let's do a bit more of this together before you go out and play.")

It's likely the way you talk to yourself is most like the first teacher. If you believe you must be hard on yourself or you will be lazy and unproductive, pay close attention to what the second teacher is doing. She demonstrates that it *is* possible to be kind while working toward your goals. You can hold yourself accountable for achieving amazing work *and* do this with warmth and kindness. What's more, this kind of feedback is energizing and motivating rather than demoralizing and overwhelming. In the following activities, you will have an opportunity to practice these qualities and in doing so continue building the skills of self-compassion.

Being Warm, Gentle, and Kind

The first step toward developing self-compassion is learning how to approach yourself *and your suffering* in a warm and understanding way. Every exercise that follows should be approached from this stance of warmth and kindness. As you try the following activities, notice the effect each one has on how you feel.

Activity: Holding Your Body with Compassion

There is a strong connection between your mind and your body. Your attitude toward your body and how you hold your body reflects how compassionately you treat yourself. To help create a posture within your body that allows for greater self-compassion, try holding your body in a compassionate way (Silberstein-Tirch 2019, Welford 2016).

Sit or stand with your body upright and straight. Find a way of standing where you feel stable and supported. If you are standing, have your feet hip-width apart and knees soft (not locked).

If you are sitting, place your feet flat on the floor, hip-distance apart, and rest your hands on your lap.

Gently roll your shoulders backward and allow them to fall away from your ears. As if being pulled gently upward, lengthen your spine, and lift your chin so that your neck, throat, and chest feel open. Loosen and soften your jaw and the space between your eyes. You may wish to have your eyes open or closed.

Allow your face to form an expression that is warm and friendly. Imagine you've just laughed at a joke, then let your face rest as it would do naturally afterward. Turn up the corners of your mouth to form a genuine smile. Allow your mind to wander toward any fond memories or comforting experiences in your past.

To increase your sense of connection to feelings of compassion, you may wish to gently place your hand on your heart or on your shoulder to give yourself a reassuring pat on the back. Alternatively, you might wrap your arms around yourself and give yourself a reassuring hug. Take a minute or two to soak up what this feels like before ending the exercise.

Write down the feelings and sensations of compassion you experienced while doing this exercise:

_____

_____

_____

Activity: Developing a Warm, Kind, Gentle Stance Toward Yourself

When people speak to you with a warm tone of voice, you will feel their care and compassion. Likewise, when people speak to you with a cold or disrespectful tone, you are likely to feel uneasy, unhappy, and defeated. The tone you use to talk to yourself in your mind makes an enormous difference to how you feel. This next exercise is adapted from one by Mary Welford (2016). In it, you will have an opportunity to hear your inner voice in different ways and notice how each feels.

Imagine you are speaking to someone for whom you feel nothing but contempt. Turn your head to the side slightly, and with a curl in your lip and a sharp tone, say the sentence "You deserve to be happy" in your mind as if you are saying it to this person. Say this twice more and each time, add a little more contempt and disgust to the tone.

Pause and notice how it feels to hear your inner voice using this harsh tone. After several moments, return to your calm, relaxed center, take a deep breath, and continue.

Now imagine you feel angry and frustrated with someone. Feel your brows knit together and your face harden as you once again say "You deserve to be happy," but this time in an angry tone. Say this twice more and each time add a little more anger and frustration to the tone.

Pause again to notice how it feels to hear your inner voice use this tone. After several moments, return to your calm, relaxed center, take a deep breath, and continue.

Finally, imagine someone for whom you feel great care and warmth. Feel your face soften and allow a gentle smile to form. Say "You deserve to be happy" one last time with noticeable warmth and a loving intention. Say this twice more, each time adding more warmth to the tone.

Pause one last time and notice how it feels to hear your own voice talking with this tone. Then take a deep breath and bring this exercise to a close.

Complete the following sentences:

The tone that most closely matches the way I speak to myself is the _____ tone.

Emotions I felt when using the warm, loving tone included _____, _____, _____, and _____.

Inner physical sensations that I experienced when using the warm, loving tone included

_____, _____, _____, and _____.

This exercise shows that it's not only what you say to yourself that matters; the tone you use inside your mind is also crucial to how you feel. By softening your tone and making it warmer and kinder, you can create a more gentle, soothing inner world for yourself.

Over the coming week (and beyond if possible), practice softening your tone of voice when you speak aloud *and* inside your mind and see if this makes a difference to how you feel.

Being Empathetic and Understanding

You may have no difficulty in being empathetic to other people's struggles. Yet, it can be extraordinarily difficult to offer this same understanding to yourself. In this next activity, you will explore how to offer *yourself* empathy and understanding. Despite how you might sometimes feel, you deserve this as much as anyone else.

Activity: Holding Your Problems Gently

Read the following script, then find a quiet place to complete this visualization at a gentle pace. If you are not fond of birds, feel free to imagine something else small, harmless, and vulnerable, such as a newborn puppy or sleeping kitten.

> As always, take a couple minutes to settle yourself into the exercise. Settle into your chair and practice Soothing Rhythm Breathing.

> Close your eyes and put your hands together to create a little bowl shape. Imagine that you are holding a baby chick in your hands. Feel the tiny bird's heart beating and its entire body trembling. Notice how you must hold this baby bird very gently in order not to hurt it in any way. Appreciate that the chick is vulnerable and how you must take extra care to hold your hands open and steady. Feel warmth and kindness flowing from you to the baby bird and allow yourself to imagine this for a minute or two.

> Now imagine you are holding your own suffering in your hands in the same way. Appreciate this as something vulnerable and needing your care. Hold your suffering gently and steadily as if you were holding the baby chick. Feel warmth and kindness flowing from you to your suffering. For several minutes, hold this kind intention toward yourself and appreciate what this feels like in your body.

> Then quietly, as you bring this exercise to a close, feel this sense of warm benevolence toward yourself and commit to carrying it with you for the rest of your day.

Briefly describe what it feels like to gently hold your own suffering, with warmth and compassion.

_____

_____

_____

At first, it may feel strange and unfamiliar to hold your own problems so tenderly. The following activity will help you develop this skill further.

Activity: Offering Yourself Peace

This activity explores what it feels like to be at peace with yourself and builds on the previous exercise. Read the following paragraphs, then guide yourself through each step at a slow and thoughtful pace. An audio file of this activity can be found at http://www.newharbinger.com/48077.

Sit comfortably and start with the slow, deep breaths of Soothing Rhythm Breathing. Feel a sense of calm and ease, allowing your eyes to close. Relax the space between your eyebrows and allow your face to form a kind, compassionate expression and your mouth to form a gentle smile. Soften in this way for a minute or two. Notice what this feels like.

Now, bring your attention to your struggle with perfectionism. Acknowledge how much you have suffered and the anxiety and stress it has caused you. For several minutes, focus your intention on holding this suffering gently and tenderly. Allow yourself several minutes to notice how this feels.

Generate within yourself a friendly, caring motivation to free yourself from suffering. Imagine your heart opening and an *intention* to offer yourself compassion, in the same way that you would offer kindness to a dear friend if they were struggling. Quietly say to yourself, using a warm tone of voice:

May you be well.

May you be happy.

May you be free of suffering.

Repeat these phrases three times, pausing after each to allow yourself to absorb the feelings of compassion. Once you are finished, notice how self-compassion feels inside your body, soaking up these sensations for several more minutes.

Then, as you gently allow this exercise to end, commit to bringing these feelings and sensations with you for the rest of your day.

Briefly describe what it feels like to offer yourself compassion in this way. On the following page, note down the emotions and sensations you experienced as you completed this exercise.

_____

_____

_____

_____

Developing a Non-Judgmental Attitude

When you struggle with unhelpful perfectionism, you may harshly and unkindly judge both yourself and your mistakes. By treating yourself with greater empathy and understanding, you can soften your attitude toward yourself and, in doing so, help soothe your overactive threat system.

Activity: Developing a Non-Judgmental Stance

This is a two-part activity. First, read the following script, and find a quiet, peaceful place to do the task. Then, take some time to answer the questions before completing the final part of this activity. An audio file of this activity can be found at http://www.newharbinger.com/48077.

Once again, start by closing your eyes or looking down toward the floor, placing your feet squarely on the ground and sitting up in your chair so that your back is straight and your head feels supported on your shoulders. Practice Soothing Rhythm Breathing to center and calm yourself before beginning.

Imagine you are sitting with a dear friend or loved one as they tell you about a problem they've been struggling with for a long time. Notice the burden this has placed on them and how much they have suffered as a result. Notice the heaviness or anxiety in your friend's voice and their feelings of sadness, frustration, and embarrassment at what has happened.

Sit alongside your friend in their distress without trying to solve their problem. Allow your friend to feel what they feel without trying to change this. Notice the intensity of your care and concern for your friend. Seek to understand their experience without judging them for their mistakes. Allow tender feelings of care and concern to flow from you to them. Stay with this experience for several minutes.

Imagine what you might say to support your friend in this moment. Then, using a warm tone of voice, imagine yourself saying this to your friend. Pause to observe the impact of your kind and non-judgmental words on your friend.

Stay with this experience for as long as you like, feeling your close connection and the desire to help your friend. Then, when you are ready, slowly open your eyes and return to the remainder of this exercise.

Write down the kind, caring, and supportive words you said to your friend here:

_____

_____

_____

Complete the final part of this activity before moving on.

Close your eyes and think about your struggle with unhelpful perfectionism. Reflect on the problems you've been having and how long you've been grappling with them.

Now, say the same words you said to your friend aloud to yourself using a warm tone of voice. Listen to the words as you say them and notice what it feels like to not harshly judge yourself but instead offer yourself acceptance. Feel a desire to help yourself through this challenging time. Pause here for a few minutes and soak in what it feels like to offer yourself compassion.

Consider what it feels like to offer yourself understanding in this way. Notice any warm, settled, and calm feelings this activity might have generated in you.

Briefly describe the emotions and sensations you experienced as you completed this exercise.

_____

_____

_____

Feeling Motivated to Help

Compassion includes the desire to help someone who is suffering, just as self-compassion means aiming to help ourselves with our struggle rather than simply judge or criticize. Instead of saying things to ourselves such as "I shouldn't let this bother me" or "I'm so pathetic for getting upset about this," you can tune in to your suffering and ask yourself, "What do I need right now?" In this next activity, you can try this out.

Activity: Offering Yourself Support in Your Efforts to Change

Read the following script, then find a quiet place to complete this activity. An audio file of this activity can be found at http://www.newharbinger.com/48077.

> Start by closing your eyes or looking down toward the floor. Slow down and deepen your breath using Soothing Rhythm Breathing. Notice the many different sensations of breathing: the gentle rise and fall of your chest, the gentle push of your lungs into your stomach, and the feeling of your lungs expanding and contracting. Allow yourself to settle into a quiet, reflective space.
>
> Think about a change you are trying to make to your unhelpful perfectionistic habits. Perhaps you want to stop procrastinating, or maybe you'd like to stop worrying so much about your friendships. Consider how hard it is to change this habit. Be curious about your struggle with this. What makes it difficult?
>
> Now consider how you could offer yourself support in this struggle. Using a warm, kind, and gentle tone of voice, ask yourself: "What do I need right now?
>
> Pause and allow your mind to generate answers to this question, considering both *practical* and *emotional* support. Allow your thoughts to flow through your mind for several minutes without needing to capture or analyze them. Then, when you are ready, open your eyes and return to complete the rest of this activity.

Write down several ways you could both practically and emotionally support yourself with this problem.

_____

_____

_____

This activity gives you a simple blueprint for starting to be more compassionate toward yourself: noticing your own experience, feeling a motivation to help, and identifying how you might do this. You may have identified some practical supports you need such as giving yourself more time or asking for help. And, you may have identified ways to emotionally support yourself such as by not criticizing yourself so much when you stumble or taking time to soothe yourself when you feel stressed or down. Whatever it is that you need, it won't help you achieve your goals unless you do it. Make a commitment to do these things you've identified. By doing so, you are being compassionate toward yourself.

Putting It Together

Being hard on yourself may be what you are used to, but it's a destructive way to live your life. You may have initially felt reluctant to change the harsh way you treat yourself, believing this will make you lazy, unproductive, or arrogant. Yet, being hard on yourself undermines your well-being and simply isn't needed to perform well. "The Two Teachers" metaphor demonstrates how it is possible to hold yourself accountable for achieving wonderful things while speaking to yourself in a warm, friendly, and supportive way. Transforming your habit of being harsh and critical of yourself into a more compassionate stance will make a noticeable difference to your life.

Our ancestors developed three emotion regulation systems that helped them find the resources they needed (drive system), respond to threats (threat system), and soothe and heal themselves (soothing system). In unhelpful perfectionism, the threat system often becomes overactive because any mistakes have become threats. The drive system may swing between being overactive as you push too hard to attain success or underactive as you give up because you feel defeated in achieving your standards. The soothing system is typically underactive and you harshly criticize yourself for your perceived failures.

Self-compassion helps bring these systems into balance. Fortunately, self-compassion is a set of skills that you can learn. These skills are the same as those you offer to others such as approaching yourself in a manner that is warm and gentle, being non-judgmental of yourself and your efforts, having empathy and understanding for your suffering, and feeling motivated to help. These skills will help you to maintain your energy and motivation while still holding yourself accountable to achieve your goals—with kindness and compassion. In this chapter, you've begun to develop these skills. In the next chapter, you will look at your tendency to be self-critical in more detail.

Taking Small Imperfect Steps: Your Personal Action Plan

Take this opportunity to develop your Personal Action Plan.

What did you learn in this chapter that was relevant to you?

1. _____

2. _____

3. _____

What did you learn about yourself?

1. _____

2. _____

3. _____

Over the coming days, what small actions would you be willing to take toward a life where your perfectionism is more helpful for you?

1. _____

2. _____

3. _____

CHAPTER 7

The Road from Criticism to Compassion

Perhaps the biggest tragedy of our lives is that freedom is possible...Yet each day we listen to inner voices that keep our life small.

—Tara Brach, *Radical Acceptance*

We live in a world defined by words. Humans use language to describe and label everything. It is through our use of language that we make sense of the world, and while it is an incredible skill that humans have, it also causes us a lot of pain (Hayes, Strosahl, and Wilson 2016). Your mind uses language to provide you with a constant stream of thoughts, both helpful and unhelpful. These thoughts include stories of the past or future, evaluations of your behavior and that of others, comparisons between yourself and other people, planning, worrying, predicting what will go wrong, and judgments of many different kinds. These thoughts can trigger your threat system and lock you into a cycle of worry, doubt, and avoidance.

When you use this amazing ability of your mind to evaluate and judge yourself, this thinking becomes destructive self-criticism. Self-criticism lies at the heart of unhelpful perfectionism. Like a relentless fault-finding machine, your perfectionistic, self-critical inner voice constantly evaluates your performance and points out every tiny error you make or could potentially make in the future.

Justin enjoyed working with numbers and liked his job as an accountant. He found it satisfying to help his clients get good tax outcomes and support their businesses. Sometimes, however, Justin got a little stuck if everything didn't balance, worrying that if things didn't add up to the last penny, he'd be seen as incompetent. Even though his boss reassured him that this detail wasn't needed, he found it hard to stop. As he looked for the source of the error, Justin was flooded with thoughts such as "I'll never get this to balance," "A more competent accountant would be able to find the error," and "I'm no good at this job." The more he had these thoughts, the more stressed he became and the harder he worked to find the mistake.

Justin experiences painful self-doubt and self-criticism. To avoid this, he works harder and harder, not letting even small inaccuracies go. Unfortunately, his self-criticism never goes away and working harder doesn't help him enjoy his work more.

Think about a mistake, big or small, that you made recently. What judgmental and critical thoughts did your mind generate? Place a checkmark against any of these statements that sound like how you would criticize yourself, your work, study, home, friendships, social life, body, or appearance. Add any other critical thoughts you might have to the end of the list.

☐ "I am useless"   ☐ "I can't do anything right"

☐ "I am incompetent"   ☐ "I will never succeed"

☐ "I am hopeless"   ☐ "I am going to embarrass myself"

☐ "I am not good enough"   ☐ "No one will like me"

☐ "I am not enough"   ☐ "I will look silly"

☐ "I'll never get better"   ☐ "I look ugly"

☐ "I am a loser"   ☐ "Other people do this better than me"

☐ "I am a failure"   ☐ "I should have done better"

☐ "I am pathetic"   ☐ "I am lazy"

☐ "I am such an idiot"   ☐ "I am a failure"

☐ "I am stupid"   ☐ "I may as well give up"

☐ "I am an imposter"   ☐ "I am broken"

☐ "I am abnormal"   ☐ "I am a bad person"

☐ "I am not important"   ☐ "I am selfish"

☐ _____   ☐ _____

☐ _____   ☐ _____

Now, look back over the list and pause for a moment to notice how uncomfortable it feels when you talk about yourself in this way. Examine the following list and check any emotions you experience when you have these thoughts. Add any extra words that reflect how you feel to the end of the list.

☐ alone	☐ grief	☐ tearful
☐ angry	☐ guilty	☐ tired
☐ anxious	☐ helpless	☐ uneasy
☐ ashamed	☐ hopeless	☐ unsure
☐ confused	☐ hurt	☐ upset
☐ defeated	☐ invisible	☐ useless
☐ dejected	☐ isolated	☐ victimized
☐ disconnected	☐ lonely	☐ worried
☐ disgusted	☐ unmotivated	☐ worthless
☐ distracted	☐ neutral	☐ _____
☐ doubtful	☐ overwhelmed	☐ _____
☐ embarrassed	☐ powerless	☐ _____
☐ fearful	☐ regretful	☐ _____
☐ foolish	☐ resentful	☐ _____
☐ frustrated	☐ sad	☐ _____

Consider how you feel inside your body when you criticize yourself. Check any of the uncomfortable physical sensations that come with self-criticism. Add any other sensations you notice to the end of the list.

- ☐ agitated
- ☐ anxious
- ☐ choked up
- ☐ churned up
- ☐ clenched
- ☐ deflated
- ☐ drained
- ☐ dulled
- ☐ empty

- ☐ exhausted
- ☐ flat
- ☐ frozen
- ☐ heavy
- ☐ numb
- ☐ on edge
- ☐ restless
- ☐ shaky
- ☐ sick/nauseous

- ☐ sweaty
- ☐ tense
- ☐ tight
- ☐ tired
- ☐ unsettled
- ☐ weary
- ☐ worked up
- ☐ _____
- ☐ _____

Now, pause again here. Consider how difficult it has been for you to manage these thoughts, feelings, and sensations for so long. I wonder how the critical way you've been speaking to yourself over all these years could have influenced your self-esteem and self-confidence, particularly if you believed the criticisms to be true. Consider how it might have undermined your confidence or fueled self-doubt, avoidance, or unhelpful habits.

Describe how self-criticism has affected you.

_____

_____

_____

_____

Take this opportunity to practice self-compassion. Allow yourself to soften as you become aware of what self-criticism has cost you. Connect with how hard this has been for you, as you would for a dear friend. Become aware of your suffering, applying your self-compassion skills, holding your experience gently, as if it was a baby bird.

Where Did You Learn to Criticize Yourself Like This?

Self-criticism doesn't just appear out of nowhere—it is a habit that is learned. So, where did you learn to speak to yourself this way? These thoughts may have come from how other people have spoken to you or from watching the way others speak about themselves. They may also be words you've generated yourself.

List any people or situations that might have contributed (intentionally or by accident) to your self-critical thinking:

_____

_____

_____

_____

_____

No matter where you've learned this style of thinking, you now use these words to hurt yourself. You've made these criticisms your own and have added to them across your life. In the next activity, we'll explore how this developed and what it might mean if you could change how you speak to yourself.

Activity: Write Your Personal History of Self-Criticism

In this activity, you will explore the history of your self-criticism and write this as a short, descriptive story. Before you begin, close your eyes, and take a few deep breaths. Practice Soothing Rhythm Breathing for several minutes until you find yourself in a calm and reflective space. Then, take your time to work through the following steps.

In your journal or on the page provided, complete this activity as if you are telling a story to someone you love and trust. Build your story from real events, but don't worry about this needing to be a complete portrayal. Draw upon the key moments. And of course, do not worry too much about spelling or grammar; focus on getting your ideas on the page.

Begin the story by describing an early memory of a time when you harshly judged yourself. Briefly explain the situation that led to this happening. To make this vivid, include details about how old you were, where this happened, who else was there, what you were doing, and even what you were wearing. Write down the critical things you said to yourself at this time. As much as you are able, connect with and describe the emotions you experienced too.

_____

_____

_____

_____

_____

_____

_____

Connect with the younger you with the same kindness and gentleness you might offer an injured animal you find on the sidewalk. What do you now know that you wish you had known back then? Feel compassion for the younger you. Using compassionate language, write down several sentences that describe your hurt and suffering.

_____

_____

_____

_____

_____

_____

_____

Now explain how your critical self-talk developed as you got older. How have you added to and elaborated on those early criticisms over time? Give examples of the kinds of things for which you criticize yourself nowadays. Describe how this has influenced the way you are living right now. What kinds of things do you avoid? What criticisms upset you the most?

_____

_____

_____

_____

_____

_____

_____

_____

Finally, end your story with a statement of hope. Write down how you'd like to change things for the better. Describe how you'd like to speak to yourself in a more encouraging and supportive way in the future.

_____

_____

_____

_____

_____

_____

_____

_____

Now that you have finished telling your story, go back and read it over from start to finish. Take a deep breath and give yourself some credit for completing this task. Remembering painful times from your past takes courage. You understand that you can't wipe away your history of self-criticism and change what's happened as a result. Nor can you unlearn the judgmental way you speak to yourself now. You can, however, learn to respond to your self-criticism with compassion and take steps in the direction of what's important. This will be the focus of the rest of this chapter.

How You Respond to Self-Criticism Matters

Self-criticism hurts. Because of this, you may have learned to fear your critical thoughts as much as you fear failure. You might be running, fighting, or hiding from your critical thoughts. The problem is that you can't escape from something in your mind; it always comes with you—and you can't defeat something that you can't control.

How you respond to your critical thoughts is important. In the following assessment, you will explore how you react to your self-critical thoughts and whether these reactions are helpful for you. Each of the following statements come from a questionnaire called the Forms of Responding to Self-Critical Thoughts (FoReST) scale, which measures how people respond to their self-criticism (White et al. 2020). You will have an opportunity to complete the final questions from the FoReST scale a little later in this chapter.

Self-Assessment: The FoReST Scale (Part 1)

Rate how true each statement is for you by circling the number next to it. Use the scale below to make your choice.

1	2	3	4	5	6	7
Never true	Very seldom true	Seldom true	Sometimes true	Frequently true	Almost always true	Always true

When I have a critical thought about myself…

Item	Rating						
…I act in a way that makes life more difficult for me.	1	2	3	4	5	6	7
…it gets me so down that I don't act in the way that I should.	1	2	3	4	5	6	7
…I don't try as hard.	1	2	3	4	5	6	7
…I waste more of my time.	1	2	3	4	5	6	7
…I don't treat myself the way I would like.	1	2	3	4	5	6	7
…I don't treat others the way I would like.	1	2	3	4	5	6	7
Total:							

If your answers are mostly 1's, 2's, 3's, and 4's and your total score is less than 24, you probably manage how you react to this reasonably well and don't let your self-criticism affect how you treat your work, yourself, or other people. However, if your answers include lots of 5's, 6's, and 7's so that your total score is greater than 24, the way you respond to self-criticism is probably causing you problems and leaving you feeling overwhelmed, on edge, threatened, and worn down.

There are several unhelpful ways that people react to their self-critical thoughts, and each offers a way to manage your self-criticism by avoiding the thoughts or neutralizing their impact. Circle any of the following approaches that you might use:

A. Analyze the thoughts: try to make sense of the thoughts and understand them better using logic and reasoning.

B. Believe the thoughts: feel hurt or devastated by the thoughts as if they are a painful truth.

C. Clash and fight with the thoughts: argue back or try to think something "positive" to eliminate, defeat, erase, or neutralize the critical thought.

D. Distract yourself from the thoughts: try to keep busy by working harder, watching YouTube, or doing anything to stop yourself from thinking these thoughts.

E. Evade and numb the intensity of the thoughts: do things to slow and quieten the thoughts such as drinking excessive alcohol, sleeping a lot, or using recreational drugs.

It's likely that you react to your self-criticism in at least one of these ways. When you look back over your lifetime, how successful has this been? Unfortunately, reacting in these ways can get you stuck in an anxiety and avoidance cycle, which may even end up making your self-criticism worse.

Now in her late-sixties, Maxine lived with her son, Pete, a veteran who had been diagnosed with post-traumatic stress disorder. In recent years, Maxine had become Pete's caregiver, supporting him through periods of deep depression that lasted several days to a week at a time. Maxine always helped him as best she could, but also learned to keep her distance from his angry outbursts. Maxine tried to keep the household calm and predictable for Pete, and one of the ways she did this was to keep regular mealtimes.

Unfortunately, after dinner, her own routines went out the window. Maxine would try to manage her chronic stress by snacking on anything she could find. At these times, her mind would also be flooded with excruciatingly loud, critical thoughts such as "I am a failure for being overweight," "Everyone can do this better than me," and "I'll never be able to control my eating." Swamped by guilt and trying to beat away the painful feelings, Maxine would argue with her critical thoughts, but she became worn out by this battle. No matter how hard she tried to think positively, Maxine never seemed to stop criticizing herself. Every time she tried to eat healthier, she would think things like "You'll never do it," "Remember you quit the last diet," "You can't stick to anything," and "You may as well give up now."

Whenever she had these thoughts, Maxine felt hopeless and defeated, believing there must be something wrong with her. Everyone else seemed to manage their thinking and eating so much better. Stuck on this self-defeating loop, the more Maxine got caught up in this thinking, the more likely she would eat to comfort herself. Trying to quiet her thoughts, Maxine let go of her health goals and struggled to keep herself from putting on weight.

Here you can see that for Maxine, arguing with her thoughts and criticizing herself for even having the thoughts contributed to a self-defeating cycle that led nowhere. Since snacking was a way of seeking comfort, it became part of this painful loop. Maxine was stuck.

Activity: Noticing Your Self-Critical Thoughts in Daily Life

This next activity will give you the foundation you need to start changing the self-critical way you speak to yourself. If you do only one activity in this chapter, please make it this one. (Obviously, I hope you'll do more.)

Your task is simple: over the next week, tune into your self-critical thoughts and write down what you hear in the space provided. Use extra pages if you like. A bonus template for this activity is available at http://www.newharbinger.com/48077 where you can log daily triggers, responses, and outcomes across a week.

For each thought, notice the trigger or situation in which the thought occurred and how you reacted to it by writing down A, B, C, D, E, or Other if you used an approach different from those listed earlier. If you notice the same thoughts over and over, make a note of that too. Self-critical thoughts can be quite repetitive.

I know that, at first, this task might feel daunting. After all, you've probably spent a lot of time and energy trying not to have these critical thoughts—and now I am asking you to pay close attention to them. It's understandable that you don't want to hear them. Yet, I can assure you that noticing your thoughts and writing them down will neither make the thoughts truer nor will they become more hurtful or painful. You are also unlikely to have more critical thoughts just because you are paying attention to them. Remember, you've been struggling to get rid of these thoughts for a long time—and yet, you still have them. If you think it might be time to try something new, try this activity.

Sample Logbook: Noticing Your Self-Critical Thoughts

[A: Analyze, B: Believe, C: Clash/Fight, D: Distract, E: Evade/Numb]

Situation	Self-Critical Thoughts	How I Reacted (A/B/C/D/E/Other)
I was attending a lecture at college.	"I am a fraud." "I'm not smart enough to do this degree."	A: I thought about how I always feel this way in class and whether I am really not smart enough. C: I tried to remind myself that I have good grades so far.
I found a mistake in a report that I'd already given to my manager.	"I am so hopeless." "I should have got this right."	B: I believed the thoughts and felt sick in my stomach.
Every night after dinner I crave chocolate.	"I'll never be able to stop eating like this." "Everyone else manages their eating better than me."	B: I believed the thoughts and felt defeated.

Logbook: Noticing Your Self-Critical Thoughts

Over the coming week, complete the following table.

[A: Analyze, B: Believe, C: Clash/Fight, D: Distract, E: Evade/Numb]

Situation	Self-Critical Thoughts	How I Reacted (A/B/C/D/E/Other)

Give yourself some credit for completing this task. This activity can be uncomfortable, so let's take stock of what you noticed.

- Underline any criticisms that are the same as others. Notice how repetitive and dull the criticisms can be.

- Make an X next to any that involve you calling yourself names such as "idiot," "stupid," or "loser." Would you speak to a friend this way?

- Place a checkmark next to any thoughts that give you useful feedback. Is there *anything* helpful in this criticism?

Then complete the following sentences:

The things I criticize myself for most are _____, _____, and _____.

I tend to respond to my self-criticism by _____ and _____.

The consequences (outcome) of this for me are _____.

Notice how the way you respond to your self-criticism can get in the way of living a life that you value.

- If you analyze your thoughts, you can get lost in a maze of reasoning that does nothing to move you toward what matters.

- If you believe your critical thoughts, it can undermine your well-being and confidence.

- If you argue with your thoughts, you can get locked into an endless arm-wrestle with your mind.

- If you distract or numb yourself, it will get in the way of doing what's deeply important for you.

By now, you may be thinking that you are a failure for the way you've been reacting to your self-criticism. If so, take a deep breath and try once again to offer yourself some compassion for this. There is a way to respond to your thoughts that works better, and you can learn how to do this using an extremely useful ACT metaphor: "The Passengers on the Bus."

Introducing "The Passengers on the Bus"

"The Passengers on the Bus" is a well-loved ACT metaphor that describes how the decisions you make in your life can either take you toward a life that you love or hold you back from progressing down the road (Hayes, Strosahl, and Wilson 2016; Stoddard and Afari 2014).

"The Passengers on the Bus" metaphor goes like this:

Imagine you are on a bus and you are the driver. This is your bus and only you can drive it; you determine the speed and direction. Down the road ahead is a life that you love: full of all the kinds of things you value such as loving relationships, satisfying and challenging work, and making a contribution to others.

Take a moment to look over the values you've identified in Chapter 4 and note down several of your most important values below. Reconnect with how energizing, rewarding, and fulfilling this life down the road would be if you were living according to these values.

_____

_____

_____

_____

On your bus are a bunch of passengers. These passengers are made up of your thoughts, emotions, bodily sensations, and memories, and they have all hopped on your bus at some point in your life. Some of these passengers are helpful and kind, and they willingly come along for the ride. They remind you of happy memories and satisfying achievements and say supportive things to you. These passengers don't bother you and you may barely even notice them.

Unfortunately, you have other passengers that are much meaner, bossier, and louder. They tell you when to turn left or right, when to stop, and when to go. One of these passengers is your Perfectionistic Self-Critic. This passenger is always evaluating and criticizing your performance. It tries to intimidate you by coming right up to the front of the bus to lean in and insult you. Its voice is cold and harsh. This passenger is persistent and can be extremely loud.

Imagine your Perfectionistic Self-Critic has come up from the back of the bus and is next to you right now. Describe what this passenger might look like in as much detail as possible.

_____

_____

_____

_____

You may like to draw your Perfectionistic Self-Critic here:

Take this opportunity to give your Perfectionistic Self-Critic a name. Try to find something that captures its essence, so you have a quick way of recognizing it when it is talking. Names I've heard before include "The Bully," "The Mean Girl," or "The Dictator." Alternatively, if nothing comes to mind, you can simply call it "The Critic" or "The Passenger."

My passenger's name is: _____

This passenger has been hanging around for a long time. It probably got on your bus in childhood or adolescence. Sometimes passengers sound like other people such as school bullies or critical family members. Remember that even if your passenger might look or sound like someone that you know, it has become the way you speak to yourself.

This passenger sounds so horrible that, naturally, you try to keep it quiet. There are several ways you might try to quieten your passenger. Let's look at each.

Doing What Your Passenger Says

First, it can seem like your passenger will stay quiet and not bother you if you just do what it says. You believe what it tells you and try to follow its instructions. You try to make a deal with the passenger, agreeing to do what it says if the passenger agrees to stay quiet. Over time, you might not even need the passenger to tell you where to go; you already know what it wants. So, when your passenger says, "Don't say anything or they'll think you are stupid" or "Check it again to make sure you haven't made a mistake," you do it without question. In the short term, this seems to work. Each time you follow the passenger's instructions, it quietens down, but it probably does not stay quiet for long.

Check with your experience. While you are busy doing what the passenger says, how much progress are you making down the road toward *your* valued future? (Circle one.)

1	2	3	4	5
No progress at all	Little progress	Slow progress	Steady progress	Rapid progress

How much of your energy does it take to do what your passenger says in this way? (Circle one.)

1	2	3	4	5
Completely exhausting	Very draining	A little tiring	Minimal effort	No effort at all

Many people tell me that doing what the passenger says doesn't take too much effort, but they also don't make much progress down the road. Describe what happens to your bus when you are following the passenger's instructions.

When I do whatever my passenger says, my bus _____

_____.

Fighting with Your Passenger

Another way to keep the passenger quiet is to fight with it. You're determined to stop it from being so critical, so you argue with the passenger, reason with it, try to outwit it using logic, or plead with it to leave you alone. You believe that if you could just win the argument, the passenger will be quiet or get off the bus.

Fighting with the passenger takes a lot of energy, and when you think about it, have you ever convinced your passenger it's wrong? Perhaps, you make a few good points, but have you ever won the argument? Does your passenger ever run out of energy? The more you fight with your passenger, the more energy and focus you are giving it. Your passenger knows how to fight, and you are playing its game. You get worn out, but your passenger does not, and for as long as you fight, you are giving it more airtime. Also notice that, to fight, the first thing you must do is take your hands off the wheel and face the passenger rather than the road.

How much progress do you make toward your valued future while you are busy fighting with your passenger? (Circle one.)

1	2	3	4	5
No progress at all	Little progress	Slow progress	Steady progress	Rapid progress

How much energy does it take to fight with your passenger in this way? (Circle one.)

1	2	3	4	5
Completely exhausting	Very draining	A little tiring	Minimal effort	No effort at all

This strategy takes a lot more effort than agreeing with your passenger, but I suspect you still don't make much progress down the road. In fact, usually neither of these strategies gets you anywhere fast. Your bus may even feel like it has stopped by the side of the road. Take a moment now to describe what happens to *your* bus when you are busy fighting your passenger.

When I fight with my passenger, my bus _____

_____.

White-Knuckling

Another common strategy I've seen people use to manage their passengers could be called "white-knuckling." White-knuckling involves gritting your teeth while you step on the gas and drive headlong down the road, pushing hard to make progress toward your valued goals. When the passenger tries to threaten or intimidate you, you actively push it away, telling it, "Shut up" or "Leave me alone," and you keep driving. To drive this way, you must have one hand tightly gripped on the wheel (giving you the white knuckles) while the other hand is pushing back the passenger. How well can you drive with one hand?

What kind of progress do you make down the road while you are white-knuckling like this? (Circle one.)

1	2	3	4	5
No progress at all	Little progress	Slow progress	Steady progress	Rapid progress

How much of your energy does it take to drive while pushing away your passenger like this? (Circle one.)

1	2	3	4	5
Completely exhausting	Very draining	A little tiring	Minimal effort	No effort at all

This white-knuckling approach is a much more difficult way to drive, but at least you feel like you are making progress, right? Unfortunately, it's often slow progress and difficult to sustain. While in the short term this strategy might take you a few miles down the road, it usually doesn't work well in the long term and you never get into cruising speed. It's also difficult to enjoy life down the road while you are busy pushing away your passenger at the same time.

The truth is that your passenger will never get off the bus, no matter which approach you use. Your passenger has been learned, and you can never unlearn them. This doesn't mean that your passenger will always cause you problems, but it does mean that it's always going to be hanging around somewhere, with the potential to cause trouble. Fortunately, there is one way you can respond to your passenger that makes a substantial difference to how much it intrudes in your life. This way of driving is called "mindful awareness" and it's time to learn this skill.

A New Way of Driving

When your passenger is being disruptive, there are some simple steps you can take that will help you make progress down the road. Imagine the following:

> You are in the driver's seat of your bus, with both of your hands on the wheel. Your eyes are focused on the road ahead. You are looking toward your valued future and a rich and fulfilling life. You are in touch with how good that life feels to you right now.
>
> On your bus with you is your Perfectionistic Self-Critic. At times, this passenger shouts at you from the back of the bus, and at other times, it comes right up to you and talks into your ear. Luckily, you know that it can't physically hurt you; all it has are words. You let those words wash over you and don't get caught up in them. You know you don't have to believe them. You know the passenger doesn't have any real power if you don't give it any.
>
> You take ownership of your role as the driver and continue to drive even in the presence of all the mean things the passenger says. You allow your passenger to hang around, don't fight it, don't react to it, and don't try to quieten it either. You don't do anything about your passenger. When your passenger gets noisy, you might simply give it a thumbs-up and kindly, warmly, and without getting into a fight say, "Thanks, but I've got this."
>
> At some point, your passenger gets particularly loud and demanding, like a toddler throwing himself on the floor of a supermarket, kicking, screaming, and demanding a candy bar. You know that if you give a toddler what he wants when he's doing this, you are rewarding his behavior, so you don't. You know eventually the toddler will stop screaming for the candy if he knows he won't receive it. And so, you keep driving.

This approach to managing your passenger is called mindful awareness. The goal of mindful awareness is to recognize and acknowledge the presence of the passenger—and to keep driving anyway. Check your own experience here: Do you often give in and do what the passenger demands? Could this be making its behavior even worse? Make a few notes about how you might approach this in the future.

_____

_____

Building the skills of mindful awareness will take practice over time. At first, it might be difficult, as the passenger can get very manipulative. Yet over time, once you focus your energy on driving and stop fighting your passenger, it is likely to quiet down. Sometimes, the passenger seems to sense you are in control and relaxes back into its seat. Sometimes, it stays loud for a long, long time. I can't predict how your passenger will respond; the only way to find out is to try it and see. Whether it gets quieter or not, you still get to make progress down the road, which is probably a better outcome than what's happening right now.

Building the Skills of Mindful Awareness

Before I describe the specific skills of mindful awareness, please complete the final part of the FoReST scale.

Self-Assessment: The FoReST Scale (Part 2)

Rate how true each statement is for you by circling the number next to it. Use the scale below to make your choice.

1	2	3	4	5	6	7
Never true	Very seldom true	Seldom true	Sometimes true	Frequently true	Almost always true	Always true

When I have a critical thought about myself…

Item	Rating						
…I can let it pass from my awareness in its own time.	1	2	3	4	5	6	7
…I notice it without getting too caught up in it.	1	2	3	4	5	6	7
…I can let the feelings it creates pass from my awareness in their own time.	1	2	3	4	5	6	7
Total:							

Answers that are mostly 1's, 2's, 3's, and 4's and a total score that is less than 12 suggests that you tend to struggle with your self-critical thoughts. Answers that include lots of 5's, 6's, and 7's and a total score that is greater than 12 suggests that you are already using some helpful strategies to manage your self-critical thoughts. Let's now explore what these are.

As the questions in the FoReST scale suggest, mindful awareness means unhooking from your critical inner dialogue and not believing or reacting to the thoughts. It also means seeing your thoughts for what they are: mental noise that your mind is constantly generating for you that is largely unhelpful and unsupportive.

In essence, mindful awareness is the ability to:

1. Let your thoughts come and go from your awareness in their own time.

2. Not get tangled in your thoughts by treating them as real or something you must act upon, but instead treat them as noise your mind gives you while you drive (like a fussing toddler in the back seat).

3. Let the uncomfortable feelings that come with the critical thoughts rise and fall in their own time without fighting them.

4. Keep doing what's important, even though your mind might tell you that you can't or shouldn't or that you might make a mistake.

By practicing mindful awareness, your thoughts will become much less of a problem in your life even if they are still there. At times you might get pulled back into the struggle with this passenger. Learning to accept the presence of your passenger in this way will take practice. This next activity will give you an opportunity to start.

Activity: Mindful Awareness of Your Critical Thoughts

In this activity, you will have an opportunity to practice the skills of mindful awareness. The first step is to go back to your logbook of self-critical thoughts and pick three self-criticisms that make you feel particularly uncomfortable. Find things your passenger would say to you quite often and write them down here:

1. _____

_____

2. _____

_____

3. _____

_____

Now, copy these three thoughts onto a small piece of paper; something small enough that you can fit it into your wallet or the back of your cell phone case. Over the next week, carry this little scrap of paper around with you. For extra points (not really), you might like to put the little piece of paper inside your shoe and walk around on it all week.

As you go about your week, don't try to change or fight your critical thoughts. Instead, every time your passenger says one of the things listed above, remind yourself that:

1. You can let the thought come and go without having to fight it.

2. Just because you have the thoughts doesn't make it real or something you need to act upon. You can treat it as background noise.

3. You can let any uncomfortable feelings that come with the thoughts pass without fighting them.

4. You can keep doing what's important even when the thoughts are loud.

Once again, acknowledge your effort in completing this challenging task. Being willing to face your uncomfortable thoughts takes courage. At the end of the week, complete the following questions.

What happened to the frequency of your critical thoughts over the week? (Circle one.)

Became more frequent   Stayed the same   Became less frequent

What happened to the intensity/painfulness of your critical thoughts over the week? (Circle one.)

Became more intense   Stayed the same   Became less intense

Consider the ways you tend to react to your self-critical thoughts, including A) analyze, B) believe, C) clash/fight, D) distract, and E) evade/numb. How did the way you reacted to these thoughts change across the week?

_____

_____

_____

_____

You may have found that the frequency and impact of your thoughts changed, even though you didn't change the content of the thoughts at all. Or, you may have found you could still do things that are important with the thoughts coming and going. The more you practice these steps to mindful awareness, the less your thoughts will interfere with how you feel and the closer you'll move toward your valued life, even if the thoughts continue to hang around.

Finding the Passenger's Good Intention

It is easier to accept the presence of your passenger if you can recognize that it has a good intention. After all, the passenger is part of you, even if it has a terrible way of trying to help you. Hating your passenger is wasted energy; it perpetuates the cycle of self-hatred and triggers your threat system further. This final practice in mindful acceptance involves considering what your passenger wants for you. Could your passenger be trying to (check one or more):

☐ Help you be successful in your pursuit of goals and achievements (by pointing out your failures, looking for potential future failures, and trying to stop these from happening)?

☐ Help you feel happy and content in yourself (by pointing out what you are doing wrong and trying to stop this, so you'll feel better)?

☐ Keep you safe from embarrassment or harm (by pointing out where you might get hurt and telling you to do certain things to keep you safe)?

Or perhaps it has some other good intention? If so, briefly describe it here:

_____

_____

_____

Your passenger currently has a destructive and unhelpful way of helping you achieve these outcomes. How do you think it might change its approach if it believed you had things under control?

_____

_____

_____

If your passenger wants you to be successful in achieving your goals, how might it behave differently if it felt confident that you (the driver) were in control of the bus, working toward a future aligned with your values?

_____

_____

_____

If your passenger wants you to be happy, criticizing you certainly is a strange way of going about it. If your passenger knew that you were focused on building a life that is aligned with your values where you would feel fulfilled, contented, and purposeful, how might it change its behavior?

_____

_____

_____

Finally, if your passenger wants to keep you safe from embarrassment, shame, or harm, how might it change its behavior if it knew that you were going to do what was best for you while taking reasonable steps to stay safe?

_____

_____

_____

When you recognize and acknowledge your passenger's good intention, can you find a little more compassion for it? In the final activity of this chapter, you'll have an opportunity to offer compassion to your Perfectionistic Self-Critic. I encourage you to complete this activity and notice how it feels.

Activity: Offering Compassion to Your Perfectionistic Passenger

Read the following script and once again find a quiet place to complete the activity and the questions that follow. An audio file of this activity can be found at http://www.newharbinger.com/48077.

Start by closing your eyes or looking down toward the floor. Notice the feeling of your body settling into your chair. Take several slow deep breaths and practice Soothing Rhythm Breathing. Let your body sink gently into the space, feeling the support of the chair and the floor, holding you in place. Feel a growing sense of ease and peace within you.

Imagine yourself sitting in the driving seat of your bus, heading down the road toward a life that you love. This life is full of the things you value such as loving relationships, satisfying and challenging work, and contributing to others and the planet. Breathe in deeply and reconnect with the sweetness of this life down the road.

On your bus with you is your Perfectionistic Self-Critic. It glares at you and comes right up to the front of the bus to insult and criticize you. It tells you what you can and can't do. Imagine this passenger in your mind's eye. Notice its posture, facial expressions, and attitude toward you. Notice the kinds of unhelpful and unkind things the passenger says to you.

Despite your efforts, this passenger is going nowhere. It is not getting off the bus. You know that fighting your passenger perpetuates the problem—you're fighting fire with fire, triggering your threat system further.

Consider what lies behind its barrage of negativity. Underneath its nasty behavior lies a good intention for you. After all, it's part of you. Maybe it wants you to be safe, free from suffering, or achieve wonderful things, but it goes about this in an unhelpful way.

Using a warm tone of voice, talk to your perfectionistic passenger in a caring way, saying:

> May you be well.

> May you be happy.

> May you be free of suffering.

Imagine compassion flowing from you to the perfectionistic passenger. If this is difficult, focus your *intention* on being compassionate to your passenger and repeat the three statements one more time. Pause here and soak up this experience for a minute or two.

Allow these images to fade from your mind's eye, bringing with you this warm feeling of self-compassion. Feel your feet resting on the floor. Your body resting on the chair. And when you are ready, open your eyes and gently return to your day, bringing with you this sense of warmth and compassion.

Take a moment right now to reflect on your experience of this mindfulness practice.

What was it like to connect with your Self-Critical Passenger in this way? What did it feel like to offer compassion to this part of yourself? Write down your thoughts below.

_____

_____

_____

_____

_____

_____

_____

_____

Putting It Together

For a long time, you've had an inner perfectionistic self-critic that has pointed out your weaknesses, called you names, and put you down. This inner voice sounds like the first teacher we discussed in Chapter 6—cold and mean—and this type of feedback gives you no room to grow. Naturally, you try to stop or get away from this critical voice.

How you respond to this self-critic matters; it determines how much progress you make toward a valued life. Believing the critical thoughts is painful *and optional.* Analyzing, fighting, trying to distract or numb yourself are common strategies, but at best, they only work in the short term.

When you visualize your self-critic as a passenger on a bus, you can see how the unhelpful ways you respond to your passenger interfere with your life. Doing what the passenger says, fighting it or white-knuckling only energizes the passenger and doesn't move you down the road.

By learning to respond to your passenger using mindful awareness, you can keep working toward a valued life *and* be kinder to yourself as you do. Mindful awareness is the ability to let your thoughts and feelings come and go from your awareness, without getting tangled in them or needing to act upon them in any way. Instead, you treat the thoughts as background noise and allow the feelings to rise and fall.

If you can find a little compassion for your Self-Critical Passenger, it is much easier to allow the passenger to hang around without reacting to it. The key is to look for the good intention that lies behind its troublesome behavior. Usually, the passenger wants you to be safe, happy, or successful in achieving your goals, even though it has a destructive way of going about it.

As you drive down the road, there will always be opportunities to gain experience from your mistakes. No one is faultless and a balanced approach is needed. Finding just the right amount of supportive self-guidance will help keep you on the road. This means giving yourself feedback that is helpful *and* is delivered with a warm, gentle, and encouraging tone of voice. By learning the crucial skill of speaking to yourself in this supportive way, you can transform your unhelpful reactions into valued action, and each day move closer to a life you find rewarding and fulfilling.

Taking Small Imperfect Steps: Your Personal Action Plan

Before you move on, take a few moments to develop your Personal Action Plan.

What did you learn in this chapter that was relevant to you?

1. _____

2. _____

3. _____

What did you learn about yourself?

1. _____

2. _____

3. _____

Over the coming days, what small actions would you be willing to take toward a life where your perfectionism is more helpful for you?

1. _____

2. _____

3. _____

CHAPTER 8

Getting Unstuck and Back on the Road

The thing that is really hard, and really amazing, is giving up on being perfect and beginning the work of becoming yourself.

—Anna Quindlen

If you have been working through this book and still find yourself getting caught up in unhelpful perfectionistic behaviors, congratulations, you are completely normal. Although you've learned some powerful tools to help you, meaningful change takes time and repetition. Hold fast. Changing your perfectionism is not a goal you can check off, and progress is not a straight line. New struggles, stresses, and life challenges will inevitably challenge you. You are likely to take one step forward and two steps backward at times.

If you are feeling stuck, it may be because your perfectionism is getting in the way of creating change. In this concluding chapter, you will explore the places you get pulled off course and how to get back on track. I will give you two more skills that will pull together what you've been learning already and help you move toward a valued life. You will explore what it means to become *more than perfect* and how to let go of stories that limit you.

But before you dive in, take some time to skim back through the pages of this book. Then, acknowledging how much work you've done so far, answer the following questions.

The activities I found most helpful were:

1. _____

2. _____

3. _____

4. _____

5. _____

Briefly describe what made these activities helpful:

_____

_____

_____

The activities that were the most challenging to complete were:

1. _____

2. _____

3. _____

4. _____

5. _____

Briefly describe what made these activities challenging:

_____

_____

_____

The activities I haven't attempted (yet) are:

1. _____

2. _____

3. _____

4. _____

5. _____

Often, the activities you find most difficult or skipped are the same ones you might benefit from most. Circle any activities listed above you will practice again or plan to do next. Perhaps, even take the time to complete some of these activities now before moving on.

Activity: Evaluating Your Progress So Far

This activity is an opportunity to acknowledge your successes. As you do, take care not to underestimate or disregard your achievements. Dismissing what you've done because it's not yet perfect or not good enough is a common unhelpful perfectionistic habit. Try not to hold yourself to unachievable standards and instead use a broad definition of success. Reshaping any long-standing habit is complex and difficult, so if you've looked at your problems differently, or tried some new ways of doing things, this is progress.

Complete the following table by describing the progress you've made toward unwinding your unhelpful perfectionistic habits and the areas where you still feel stuck. It may help to look back over your responses to the checklist of "Common Unhelpful Perfectionistic Behaviors" in Chapter 1 and notice anything that has improved for you. You might also review your answers to "Identifying Your Most Unhelpful Habits" in Chapter 5.

Habits that have changed for the better	
Habits that are starting to improve	
Habits where I still feel stuck	

If you don't feel you are making *any* progress, pause for a moment and consider: Are your standards for progress still too high? Have you tried doing at least one thing differently? Acknowledge any tiny shifts toward more helpful perfectionism and add them to the table above.

Consider what has helped you make progress so far. Did you:

- Set, clear, specific, and flexible goals where you could improve over time?

- Make a firm decision to stop doing something that wasn't helping you?

- Realign your behavior toward your values?

- Stop listening to your Self-Critical Passenger and take control of the bus?

- Do what was important even though it was uncomfortable?

- Get help from friends, family, or a licensed therapist?

Complete the following sentence, writing down as many different ideas as you can:

I have made positive changes in my life by:

_____

_____

_____

_____

_____

Take this moment to appreciate what has gone well. Whatever this is, keep doing it! For the areas where you still feel stuck, let's examine why this might be the case.

Getting Unstuck

There are three broad ways you might be derailed in your efforts to change unhelpful perfectionistic habits. Unfortunately, it is often the same unhelpful perfectionistic habits that you are trying to change that get in the way. Making small adjustments to your approach will help you make greater progress.

Fine-Tune Your Goals for Success

Even when you know how to set effective goals, it can still be difficult not to approach goals in a perfectionistic way. As you read through the following section, look for small ways you can tweak your goals to increase your chances of success. The best kind of goal is the one you actually do.

Overly ambitious goals. The single most common mistake perfectionists make is to set goals that are too big and too vague. Goals like "be more confident socially" or "find better work-life balance" might describe what you want to achieve, but to be more effective, you'll need to break them down into smaller steps. Checking off smaller steps will help you stay motivated too. It can be surprising just how small your steps must be to be achievable. Big, ambitious goals may promise a leap to the finish line, but without doing the boring work of changing your small, unhelpful perfectionistic habits, it will rarely work. Despite what you may believe, goals that are relatively easy to do are usually the most effective in creating change, primarily because you are more likely to do them.

Negative goals. When goals are descriptions of what *not* to do, they are difficult to achieve. You are left wondering what to do next. If you aim to "stop procrastinating," what are you actually going to *do?* Defining your valued goals and breaking them down into practical steps will make your task much easier. You can focus your efforts on what's really going to help and not waste your time. So, to stop procrastinating, you might focus on your values, plan your time thoughtfully, break your work into smaller tasks, learn to refocus when you get anxious or overwhelmed, or seek support to help you stay on task. Focusing your efforts on practicing these skills will help you overcome procrastination by moving you toward values like making better use of your time, being more productive, or handing in good quality work.

Goals that demand perfection. Do you expect yourself to stop your unhelpful habits starting today, and plan for this to continue every day that follows? If so, this is not realistic. To build more helpful habits, your goals need to clearly define your desired actions and you need to increase the frequency of these behaviors *over time*. Through many small steps repeated over and over, you can transform unhelpful perfectionistic habits. Messing up is an essential part of this process as it helps you make adjustments and reminds you to stay on task. If you are working toward being more efficient in completing your work, the times when you get distracted or waste valuable time can form powerful reminders of how important it is to practice staying focused. Noticing the pain in these moments (in a compassionate way) can help you to refocus and get on track again.

Goals not aligned to values. Remember to align your goals with your values. If you are working toward a goal because it reflects how you should be or because it's what someone else wants, it won't motivate you. Look for what you value and adjust your goal accordingly. Sometimes, a goal aligns with one of your values but also competes with another important value. Somehow, you must find a way to reconcile these two competing values just as Charlie has in the example below.

> *Charlie wanted to work less and spend more time with his kids. He knew they were growing up fast and wanted to be an important part of their lives. But, he also knew that he needed to keep his job to support his family. His boss was demanding and his role was hectic. Charlie felt torn between two important values: being an engaged and caring father and supporting his family. He realized there was no perfect answer to this. Not feeling completely comfortable about what to do, Charlie found a compromise: He focused on giving his kids his full attention in the evenings and weekends and made a commitment to finish early on Fridays to take his daughter to play T-ball. He also started to look for another job that would give him greater flexibility. He knew it might take a while for things to improve, but by taking these steps, he felt like he was on the way.*

Charlie found a compromise that helped him to move in a direction aligned with his values. While he couldn't do all the things he wanted, Charlie felt motivated by his choices and satisfied that he was doing his best.

Now, take a moment to consider where you could be going wrong with your goals. Check any of the following that might be problems with your goals:

- ☐ Too big

- ☐ Too vague

- ☐ Attempt to leap to the finish line (too ambitious)

- ☐ Focus on what to stop, not what to *do*

- ☐ Demand perfect performance

- ☐ Not aligned with your values

- ☐ In conflict with other values

Staying on track involves setting goals that are small, doable, clearly defined, and highly valued. When your actions are clearly defined and aligned to your values, you can return to the same helpful steps each time you get off track. Complete the following sentence.

I can make my goals more targeted, effective, and motivating by _____

_____

_____

_____.

To get yourself back on track, choose one small helpful action and *start doing it now.* Find something you can readily achieve *most of the time* and it will give you a solid foundation for improvement and the chance to build on your success. Complete the following sentence.

The one small helpful action I will start *right now* is _____

_____.

Overcome Perfectionistic Patterns

Do you intend to do the exercises in this book, but haven't quite done them yet? Perhaps, you are trying to change your perfectionism in such a way that you'll feel certain your approach won't be wrong. Maybe you struggle to decide what to do, not wanting to make the wrong choice. If you are having any of these problems, then your unhelpful perfectionistic habits are getting in the way of your progress.

Sandy knew she was perfectionistic and that she needed to change. She tended to work too hard and take on too much, leaving her feeling burned out. Sandy worried that her manager would be unhappy with her if she didn't work so hard. Each week, at the team meeting, Sandy would offer to take on extra projects, adding to her already heavy workload. Sandy decided that she needed to delegate the mundane work to junior team members; however, after handing over a spreadsheet to someone else to complete, Sandy found herself feeling uneasy, worried about whether it would be done properly. Sandy decided it would be better to check the spreadsheets herself before handing them over, so she could put her mind at ease. Feeling relieved by this compromise, Sandy promised herself she'd take more active steps toward lightening her workload another day.

In her attempts to change her behavior, Sandy quickly fell back into unhelpful perfectionistic patterns. Checking the work before handing it to someone else might have reassured her, but didn't save her any time, lighten her workload, or reduce her feelings of burnout.

Which of the following perfectionistic patterns could be getting in the way of your progress? Check any that apply.

☐ Trying to do things without making any mistakes

☐ Having difficulty deciding what needs to change

☐ Feeling scared to try something new because it might not be "right"

☐ Procrastinating on applying new skills

☐ Trying to do too much, too quickly, in a rush to the finish (and attempt to avoid the messy middle)

☐ Starting again to make sure it's right in an endless "do-over"

☐ Avoiding looking at the problems at all

Each of these behaviors is a way of protecting yourself from the discomfort and uncertainty that comes when you try to change perfectionistic habits. You might find the process of change:

- Too frightening and overwhelming

- Too confusing and uncertain

- Too physically uncomfortable (sick, churning, or tense sensations)

- Like you'd lose some part of yourself

- Like you'd have to change who you are

- Too uncomfortable, like there's something wrong with you

If you are feeling this way, then the change you are trying to make might be too ambitious. After all, having to alter long-standing perfectionistic habits implies you must have been doing something wrong. This alone can be difficult to accept as a perfectionist, bringing up the painful feelings associated with failure such as sadness, regret, loss, and shame. Notice also whether you criticize the way you've approached this book and feel like a failure. There is your perfectionism yet again.

Please take a deep breath right now. If you are caught in any of these perfectionistic traps or are finding the process of change just too confronting, I encourage you to get back to basics and offer yourself some compassion. Focus on the small, tangible steps you can take. Notice the emotions and uncomfortable sensations that come with these, and for short periods of time, allow yourself to experience this. Remember that the end of this book is only the start of your journey. You can keep going, and still have a lot you can gain from here. And, if you still find yourself feeling completely stuck, remember to seek help from a licensed therapist.

Describe how you could create positive changes for yourself in a way that is *more flexible* and *less perfect:*

_____

_____

_____

_____

_____

Make Peace with the Perfectionistic Passenger

One of the most common reasons why people struggle to change their unhelpful habits comes from how they respond to the criticism coming from their Self-Critical Passenger. Your passenger will go all out to achieve what it wants for you, even if it leaves a trail of destruction in its wake. In trying to help you achieve your goals, it will say things like, "Work harder," "Don't be so lazy," and "Fix yourself" to make sure you don't make a mistake. To keep you safe from failure, your perfectionistic passenger will tell you that "Change is too difficult," and "You won't succeed" until you stop.

You can quickly get pulled into unproductive ways of responding to the perfectionistic passenger, believing it, doing what it says, arguing with it, or trying to push through while keeping the passenger quiet (white-knuckling). If you believe your passenger and do what it says, you will struggle to keep going. If you fight with your passenger or try to white-knuckle your way through, you'll find the process of change exhausting and may even give up.

With practice, you can learn to let your passenger come along for the ride *and* get on with driving your bus, even if the passenger is extremely loud, hurtful, and persistent. Using your skills in mindful awareness, you can learn not to give the passenger any attention and keep going.

Describe how you could respond to your perfectionistic passenger in more constructive ways.

_____

_____

_____

_____

_____

Harnessing Your Ability to Choose

For a long time, you've been reacting to the things that scare you (mistakes, failure, embarrassment) so fast that it's become automatic and habitual. Yet, you *can* choose how you respond to the world around you, including the things you find uncomfortable, if you deliberately slow down and pay attention long enough to make an active choice. The moment immediately before your reaction to a situation is sometimes called the "Choice Point" (Ciarrochi, Bailey, and Harris 2014). In this moment, you can either take an automatic, unhelpful action *away* from your values or decide to step mindfully *toward* your values. Within the decision to move toward or away lies your personal freedom. Living this way requires effort and persistence (Walser 2019) and there are two skills that will help you put this into action in a more consistent way: willingness and curiosity. You can think of each of these skills like muscles you can strengthen. In each moment is a new opportunity to practice.

Approaching Your Life with Curiosity

Picture a small child the first time they see a rainbow. I can't help but smile when I imagine the expression of pure wonder on their face. From the first year of life, young children have a wide-eyed curiosity about the world. Unfortunately, by the time we reach adulthood, many of us have often lost touch with our ability to be curious. Curiosity isn't always encouraged in adults. You may need to step into completely unfamiliar environments, such as when you travel, to re-experience this wonder and curiosity.

Curiosity means stepping back from your expectations and exploring your experiences as if you are that small child. Curiosity is a useful skill to explore our inner world too. You can build your capacity to be curious, and the more you use it, the easier it is to access it when you need it (Sedley and Coyne 2020). You've started building this skill already through every exercise in this book where you noticed and labeled your inner thoughts, emotions, and inner sensations. You've been curious about the way you respond to failure and your struggles with the passenger on the bus. Here are some more opportunities to practice.

Activity: Developing the Wonder and Curiosity of a Small Child

In this activity, you will extend curiosity to both your external and internal worlds.

Part 1: Curiosity and Wonder at the World Around You

If you are able, step outside or go to a window.

If you can see trees or plants, notice how many different shades of green you can see. Notice how different the greens can look in the shade versus in the sun. Find shades of green that are close to yellow and others that are close to brown.

If you are in an urban environment, notice how many shades of red you can see. Notice how different red can look in the dark versus in the light. Find shades of red that are close to brown and others that are close to pink.

Spend several minutes quietly contemplating what you can see. As you do so, find at least three things that you've never noticed in your outside world before. Pause on each and acknowledge their presence. Feel a sense of appreciation for the complexity and beauty of the natural and urban worlds.

Part 2: Curiosity and Wonder for Your Body

Look at your thumb as if you've never seen it before. Notice areas of lighter, darker, browner, or pinker skin. Notice the quality of your skin; the veins, wrinkles, and creasing on your knuckles. Consider how much your thumb has been through already and how your thumb's history is written in freckles, spots, or scars. Pause here for several minutes and appreciate all the ways your thumb helps you.

Part 3: Curiosity and Wonder for Your Inner World

Close your eyes and extend your curiosity to the organs inside your chest. In it is the same heart that started beating in your mother's womb and it has been beating for you ever since, pumping harder when you've been hiking or been anxious and slower when you've been resting and relaxed. Imagine your heart beating right now, circulating blood around your body with a steady rhythm. Notice this constant movement and experience appreciation and wonder for your heart.

Contemplate your capacity to be curious. List several areas in your life where you could practice your skill of curiosity and continue to strengthen this skill.

_____

_____

_____

_____

Being Willing to Be Uncomfortable

It may surprise you to hear that the aim of this book is not to simply make you feel better; after all, this is what your unhelpful perfectionistic habits have been trying to achieve without success. Instead, I have encouraged you to become *willing* to have the full experience of life, even the unwanted and uncomfortable parts, in order to live a life that is meaningful for you and much more than perfect. If you keep trying to get rid of uncomfortable feelings or experiences through the activities you are doing or goals you've set, you are unlikely to succeed in making positive change. Only by willingly embracing the messiness and imperfection of both life *and you* can you move beyond the limits that perfectionism is placing on you. Your willingness to feel *everything* is the key.

A few things you might not know about willingness. First, it is not giving up or giving in, and it certainly isn't just tolerating things you don't like while wishing they would go away. Willingness is whole-heartedly leaning into the prickles of life, knowing that with them you also find beautiful flowers.

Willingness is not something you can compromise on. You can't be "fairly willing" or "moderately willing." Willingness has an all-or-nothing quality to it (Hayes, Strosahl, and Wilson 2016). Sometimes, you might talk about becoming more willing. However, willingness is not a dial you can turn up and down—it's more like a switch. At any given point, you are either willing or not. Fortunately, this means there's always an opportunity to switch on your willingness.

Being willing is not easy. When things scare us, our natural urge is to get away, fight even harder, or hide. These responses are programmed into our emotion regulation systems and ultimately keep us alive. However, mistakes, failure, and embarrassment are not the real-life tigers that our early ancestors faced on the savannah (even though your body may respond as if they are), and with practice, you can respond differently. Being willing to feel fear gives you an opportunity to move toward what's important rather than away from the thing that scares you.

Activity: Are You Willing?

This activity has been adapted from a book for treating OCD called *Stuff That's Loud* by Ben Sedley and Lisa Coyne (2020). Below are listed several tasks that form small practices in willingness. Doing them will build your willingness to feel uncomfortable. Some of these tasks might be easy for you, others incredibly difficult. You can add to this list if you like. I challenge you to do one or more of these tasks every day for a week. Check off each item as you complete it.

☐ Wear mismatched socks all day

☐ Go to the gym with your shirt turned inside out

☐ Eat a new food you've never tried

☐ Eat something you know you don't like

☐ Smile at a stranger

☐ Listen to a style of music you normally don't listen to such as jazz, classical, or heavy metal

☐ Delete all your social media apps and unplug for two days

☐ Leave one bite of food on your plate

☐ Ask your boss for feedback *and listen to what they say*

☐ Wear something inappropriate such as a ball gown to the store or suit to the football game

☐ Take a different route to school or work

☐ Sit in a different chair at dinnertime

☐ Try a new sport, or go kick a ball

☐ Sing karaoke

☐ Speak up in a meeting

☐ Stand in the rain without an umbrella

☐ Go out without putting on makeup or brushing your hair

☐ Set your alarm thirty minutes earlier *and get out of bed* for no specific reason

Think about your current capacity for willingness. List several more areas in your life where you could develop your willingness to try new things or be uncomfortable.

_____

_____

_____

_____

Moving Toward What Matters

In this book, you've set several goals to change your unhelpful perfectionistic behavior with each goal designed to move you toward your values. Lasting change means putting your valued goals into action day after day. At times, you'll lose your way and need to make a "gentle return" to your valued path. In this way, each decision is an opportunity to move *toward* your values or *away* from what is important. Life consists of many such moments, and over time, by using your values as a compass to guide you, you can make small moves toward your values that change the entire direction of your life.

The following activity is an opportunity to see your goals as part of a bigger shift toward your values. *Being curious* will help you tune in to your experiences and help you make these decisions in the moment. Being *willing* to have uncomfortable experiences will help you take action.

Activity: Moving Toward Your Values

Complete the worksheet below using the step-by-step instructions and example provided. You can also download a copy from http://www.newharbinger.com/48077.

Start by writing your values at the top of the sheet. Briefly describe several elements of a valued life for you: a life that will motivate and inspire you to change things for the better.

Complete the left-hand side of the sheet first. Your "away moves" are what you are currently doing that is taking you away from a life that you love. These will include your unhelpful perfectionistic behaviors and anything else you do that keeps you from living a valued life.

Below this is a space to note down the inner experiences, both comfortable and uncomfortable, that show up with these away moves. Take this opportunity to be curious. Write down any comments your passenger might make and any emotions or physical sensations that could appear along with the away moves.

Next, complete the right-hand side of the sheet. Think about what would move you toward a life that you love, aligned with your values. Your "toward moves" are things that, if living a life that you love was on the line, you would be *willing* to do. They may also be valued goals. List as many possible moves as you can on the right-hand side, including some more challenging moves for the future.

Underneath this is a space to explore the inner experiences, both comfortable and uncomfortable, that come with toward moves. This is your second chance to be curious. Write down any comments your passenger might make and any emotions or inner experiences that you anticipate happening.

Worksheet: Moving Toward Your Values (Example)

Your Values:

Having a loving relationship; being a warm, playful, and energetic mom; supporting my friends; making a contribution to the community through my work; and feeling financially secure.

Away Moves: What actions take you away from your values?	**Toward Moves:** What actions take you toward your values?
"Being overly critical of my husband."	"Taking time to connect with my husband and go out for dinner once a month."
"Working long hours and not seeing my kids."	"Spending more time playing with the kids."
"Trying to keep the house tidy at all times."	"Focusing on doing great work for my clients, especially when I feel frustrated with the management."
"Not telling my boss about my new project ideas."	"Building relationships with my colleagues by asking them out to lunch."
"Eating lunch at my desk, feeling frustrated with the management of the company."	
What Shows Up	**What Shows Up**
Critical things the passenger might say:	Critical things the passenger might say:
"No one wants to spend time with you anyway."	"It's not going to be enough."
"You are a terrible mother."	"This is too hard; you can't do it right."
Accompanying emotions and sensations:	Accompanying emotions and sensations:
sadness, frustration, guilt, regret, shame	sadness, fear, apprehension, frustration

Worksheet: Moving Toward Your Values

Your Values:	

Away Moves: What actions take you away from your values?	**Toward Moves:** What actions take you toward your values?
1. _____	1. _____
2. _____	2. _____
3. _____	3. _____
4. _____	4. _____
5. _____	5. _____
6. _____	6. _____
7. _____	7. _____
8. _____	8. _____
9. _____	9. _____
10. _____	10. _____

What Shows Up	What Shows Up
Critical things the passenger might say:	Critical things the passenger might say:
Accompanying emotions and sensations:	Accompanying emotions and sensations:

Look back over your completed worksheet and notice how both comfortable and uncomfortable thoughts, emotions, and physical sensations show up, no matter which direction you take. This prompts me to ask:

If you are going to feel uncomfortable either way, which direction will you choose?

With the power to choose your direction comes personal responsibility. You cannot blame your unhelpful habits on your situation, certain triggers, or other people. It is you who sits behind the wheel and it is you who decides your speed and direction. By noticing what shows up with curiosity and being willing to be uncomfortable in the process, you can make choices that steer your life toward what matters. The process of change can then be distilled into one simple question:

"Is what I am doing in this moment moving me toward my values?"

Becoming More Than Perfect

Transforming your perfectionism into something new can feel weird and unfamiliar. When you've been doing things the same way for a long time, your habits can become ingrained in who you are. Changing your behavior means seeing yourself in a new way, yet you may initially feel reluctant to alter habits in ways that don't feel like "you." For example, if you work hard to get good results and avoid mistakes, you may have come to see being a "hard worker" as an important part of who you are and be reluctant to take a break. In this section, you will explore how you see yourself, how these stories can define and constrain you, and how to hold them more lightly. Doing so will provide you with the space to become much more than perfect.

Activity: Who Am I? (Part 1)

This activity has been adapted from the book *Living with Your Body and Other Things You Hate* by Emily Sandoz and Troy DuFrene (2013). Here, you are going to complete it in two parts, starting with a pen and paper exercise.

Below you will find the phrase "I am…" written thirty-six times. Set a timer for three minutes and then when you are ready, take a deep breath and start the timer. Your task is to complete as many sentences as you can in the time allowed. Only stop when the timer is finished or you have completed all thirty-six sentences, whichever comes first. There are no correct answers—just go for it.

1. I am…	19. I am…
2. I am…	20. I am…
3. I am…	21. I am…
4. I am…	22. I am…
5. I am…	23. I am…
6. I am…	24. I am…
7. I am…	25. I am…
8. I am…	26. I am…
9. I am…	27. I am…
10. I am…	28. I am…
11. I am…	29. I am…
12. I am…	30. I am…
13. I am…	31. I am…

14. I am…	32. I am…
15. I am…	33. I am…
16. I am…	34. I am…
17. I am…	35. I am…
18. I am…	36. I am…

Once the three minutes are over, close your eyes, take a few deep breaths, then look back over what you've written. Scan your answers and see if it is made up of statements with:

- Facts such as your age, sex, or height

- Self-criticisms and judgments

- Stories you have about who you are

- Things other people say about you

- Stories about how you are not good enough

- Stories about how you must be exceptional

- Things that seem to conflict with other things you've listed

- Things that only apply in some situations

- Things that don't really fit, now that you look at them

You have collected stories about yourself across your entire life, built upon your own experiences and the way that others describe you. These well-developed stories define who you are, why you are that way, what you are good at, and what you can't do. I suspect I have merely scratched the surface of your opinions about yourself.

These stories can exert powerful control over your behavior. Sometimes, the stories might drive you in helpful ways. However, no matter what your stories are, any time you treat them like rules, your options will narrow. The stories become "word prisons" that define and limit you (Twohig, Levin, and Ong 2021, Wilson and DuFrene 2012) and become woven into the self-criticism provided by your perfectionistic passenger. These prisons are most difficult to escape when you believe the stories are true and they define what you do.

Muhammad worked as a typesetter and loved both the creativity and exactness of this job. He was fast and efficient, his employer was always happy with his work, and he was well-respected by his team. As he grew up, Muhammad's parents had emphasized the importance of being quiet, respectful, and hardworking, and told him to never rock the boat. Consequently, Muhammad felt deeply uneasy whenever someone challenged authority or caused conflict. So, when his manager asked Muhammad to support a newer member of the team, he was happy to help, despite having some large projects on his plate. He dutifully checked over their work and fixed the problems he found. Muhammad quickly realized this person did not have the accuracy needed to do the job well; however, believing that he couldn't cope with conflict, Muhammad did not report this to his manager. Instead, he kept fixing this person's work for months, in addition to his own heavy workload.

Muhammad's belief that he cannot cope with conflict prevented him from resolving this issue and kept him stuck. "I can't handle conflict" is just one of the many self-critical stories I've heard over the years. Here are some others.

"I am not a confident person" (one of mine)   "I'm too loud"

"I am too shy to ask someone out"   "I'm annoying"

"I am not good in relationships"   "I'm broken"

"I am socially awkward"   "I'm a bad friend"

"I am quite lazy"   "I am too critical"

Notice how unhelpful these stories can be. Yet, each was believed to be true. Knowing this, it is now time to complete the second part of the activity. Here you will explore how tightly you hold on to your stories about yourself and what it could mean to let them go.

Activity: Who Am I? (Part 2)

First, look back over your thirty-six "I am" statements. Is this list a complete description of who you are? If you were to show this list to someone who hasn't met you before, would they *know* you? I doubt it. Your list might describe you, but *it isn't you*.

Identify those statements to which you feel most attached. Some just feel more like you than others. Underline the statements you hold on to tightly in this way. Notice how the statements you've underlined might define how you behave in certain situations. Some might reflect the best version of yourself and what you are striving for. Others may be important roles you play in your life, such as being a mom or brother. Some are things you simply believe to be true. And yet others are self-descriptions that are undermining, dismissive, or critical, yet you may still hold on to them tightly. You may even feel the need to defend them even though the story you are defending isn't helpful for you (Walser 2019). In this activity, you can explore just how tightly you hold some of your stories.

Now, find a quiet place to complete the following self-reflection activity. Settle yourself into your chair with your list of "I am" statements and a pen or pencil in front of you.

Start by practicing Soothing Rhythm Breathing for several minutes. When you are in a calm and reflective space, take a deep breath and draw a line through the statement you've written against number 8. Strike it out slowly and mindfully. As you do, imagine that this statement no longer described you or reflected who you are. *Let it go.* Watch what happens inside yourself as you do this, noting any emotions such as uneasiness, confusion, or doubt as they arise. Even if it is tricky to let go of this statement, take a deep breath and continue.

Now repeat the process. Except, this time, draw a line through the statements numbered 6 and 12. *Again, imagine these no longer describe you.* Let them go too. Again, notice any emotions that emerge as you do this. You may feel relief or resistance within yourself as you let these parts of yourself go. If you have drawn through any of the strongly held statements you underlined earlier, pay close attention to how it feels to let these go too. Take several more slow, deep breaths before moving on.

Continue the same way, slowly crossing out the statements numbered 2 to 5, then 15 and 20. Take your time, letting each go in turn. Pause after each to watch your reactions and note any attachment you feel to these statements. Some statements will feel easier to let go of than others.

Then finally, strike out *all* the remaining items. Imagine they no longer define who you are. Continue to breathe, noticing all the complex emotions that come with letting these go.

Become aware of the limits in the way you describe yourself. Your stories can never fully define who you are; there is always a *you* that is more than your stories. Part of you is watching your reactions and emotions and noticing your thoughts. This part stays constant even when your stories about yourself change. Take a moment to acknowledge this "observing self" at the center point of you. Finally, take several deep breaths and return to your day, bringing with you the awareness that your self will always be greater than how you are defined by yourself and others.

You do not have to be defined by the stories you have of yourself. *You are not these stories,* so hold them lightly, just like all the unhelpful things your passenger says (Wilson and DuFrene 2012). By applying the same mindful awareness skills that you learned in Chapter 7, *you* can decide how much your stories define who you are and what you can do. When the story is useful for you, go ahead and listen to it. When it is unhelpful, politely ignore it (Twohig, Levin, and Ong 2021) or simply let it be. You do not have to be defined by the perfectionistic rules, personal standards, or limitations held within these stories.

In the final worksheet within this book, take stock of your own word prisons. Examine how each story can limit you. Make a commitment to living differently by noting down ways you can behave that are inconsistent with these limitations. Describe how you might "break out," operating outside the rules and living according to your values. You can use the worksheet provided in this book or download a copy from http://www.newharbinger.com/48077 .

Example Worksheet: Building Flexible Self-Stories

My Self-Story	How This Story Limits Me	Ways I Can Act Inconsistently with This Story
"I can't cope with conflict."	I put up with a lot of backchat and rudeness from my children until I eventually explode.	I can pause, take a deep breath, and remind my kids not to speak to me rudely. I can use a calm but firm tone. I can follow through with consequences if they don't change their behavior.
"I am too lazy."	I try to show that I'm not lazy to myself and other people by always working hard.	I can take some time off and go to the beach or read a novel. I can arrange a catch-up with my friends.
"I am a quiet person."	I don't say anything when my colleague talks over me in meetings.	I can politely but firmly restate what I was saying in the meeting. I can remind my manager that we all need a chance to contribute.
"I am socially awkward."	I don't call my old friends because I don't think they'll want to spend time with me.	I can invite my friends to come over for a pizza night.

Worksheet: Building Flexible Self-Stories

My Self-Story	How This Story Limits Me	Ways I Can Act Inconsistently with This Story

Putting It Together

In this chapter, you've looked back over the work you've been doing and you've evaluated your progress so far. You've found things that have improved and areas where you feel stuck. I hope you took this opportunity to acknowledge what you've achieved.

There are several common ways that perfectionists get stuck making changes. You may have set goals that are too ambitious, too vague, or not aligned with your values. Maybe you got pulled into perfectionistic patterns such as procrastinating, avoiding things that are uncomfortable, or got into a fight with your perfectionistic passenger. Taking small, valued steps that are readily achievable and purposefully take you toward what is important can help break this impasse.

By lifting up your view from the detail and looking at where you are going more broadly, you can begin to see your goals as part of a bigger shift toward what's important; a transformation achieved via small steps taken each day. Simply asking yourself, "Is what I am doing in this moment moving me toward what is important?" allows for moment-by-moment choices to redirect your life toward something more fulfilling, using your values as a compass to guide you.

Along the way, who you are will change in positive ways. Holding on to old habits and stories about yourself will restrict you to choices you made in the past and hold you back. You do not have to behave in ways that are consistent with the old stories you have about yourself. Seeing yourself as much more than these stories will give you greater room to grow and become much more than "perfect."

Taking Small, Imperfect Steps: Your Personal Action Plan

Take this opportunity to develop your final Personal Action Plan. Use this opportunity to consider what steps you will take you toward a more helpful perfectionism that works better for you.

What did you learn in this chapter that particularly resonated for you?

1. _____

2. _____

3. _____

What did you learn about yourself in this chapter?

1. _____

2. _____

3. _____

Over the coming months, what would you most like to change about your unhelpful perfectionism?

1. _____

_____

2. _____

_____

3. _____

_____

Over the coming days and weeks, what changes would you like to make to your habits that, if you were to keep doing them, would move you toward a life where your perfectionism is more helpful?

1. _____

_____

2. _____

_____

3. _____

_____

Living Your Best (Yet Imperfect) Life

Happiness cannot be pursued; it must ensue.

—Viktor Frankl, from *Man's Search for Meaning*

This book is just the start of your journey toward more helpful perfectionism and building a life that you love. My journey has taken years, and it's still going. I still get caught in unhelpful patterns at times. I hope that by passing on the skills I've learned from Acceptance and Commitment Therapy and Compassion-Focused Therapy, the route will be a little less bumpy for you, but it won't be without backward steps. I've realized that there is no end point to this adventure; no destination where my perfectionism doesn't have the potential to be a problem for me. I expect it to be the same for you. Under times of pressure and stress, old habits creep back in. Learning to recognize these moments is the key.

Somewhere along the road, you got off track, learning habits that have taken you to some uncomfortable places. Fighting difficult feelings has kept you stuck, unable to move toward the things that matter to you. Yet, there is nothing wrong with you. You, *and your difficult feelings,* are not a problem you need to solve. No one here needs to be fixed. So, it's time to stop beating yourself up for your mistakes. This only perpetuates a cycle of running, fighting, and hiding and it achieves nothing. Being angry at yourself for your unhelpful perfectionism will get you nowhere. The *you* that got stuck in these habits *back then* is the same you that has an opportunity to change things *now*. Both *you then* and *you now* deserve compassion. Fortunately, *you now* can offer it. Moving toward what matters will be much easier when you treat yourself with warmth, kindness, and understanding.

What you do from here matters. My hope is that you find a way to lean into the things that scare you. You'll find that your mistakes now are not the saber-toothed tigers that your ancestors faced. You *can* open up to difficult feelings with mindful awareness and find the strength and determination to move toward what matters without fighting your difficult feelings. I know this will take practice. You'll mess up and fall back into old habits again and again. Making a change for the better will take effort and persistence. And, you'll never arrive at a final, perfect destination. Your life is an ongoing process (Walser 2019), and in every moment, there is an opportunity to make a choice to move toward or away from what matters. What you choose to *do* will create meaning and value in your life. Some actions might be tiny; some might be momentous, even if you don't realize it at the time. As you change, your relationships with others, your work, and every aspect of your life will change too.

The effort will be worth it. Living fully and purposefully, including all the messiness of life, will open up your life in many amazing ways. Your worth will be no longer be tied to high grades or the approval of others. As you live according to your values, you'll feel more fulfilled, contented, deeply connected to the people in your life, and satisfied that you are contributing in important ways. I hope this book helps you live your best, imperfect, life. Thank you for sharing part of your journey with me. Good luck with your journey from here.

Acknowledgments

I always secretly wanted to write a book, but just like so many great things, it takes a village to make it a reality. To my husband, Travis, thank you for picking up *all* the slack while I worked on this project. Your support made this possible. I am so grateful that you believed I had something of value to say and encouraged me to say it. To my publishing team at New Harbinger (Tesilya Hanauer and Jennifer Holder, in particular), I have appreciated your much-needed encouragement and support. Thank you for helping me find my voice and being available to answer the simplest of questions for this budding author. To the amazing Lisa Coyne, it means so much that you were willing to add your words of wisdom to my first book. Thank you for having faith in me. Finally, a shout-out to all my friends in the contextual behavioral science community: there are too many of you to name. You continue to inspire and encourage me in all the work I do. Warmest thanks to you all.

References

Bandelow, B., and S. Michaelis. 2015. "Epidemiology of Anxiety Disorders in the Twenty-First Century." *Dialogues in Clinical Neuroscience* 17(3): 327–35.

Burgess, A., R. O. Frost, C. Marani, and I. Gabrielson. 2018. "Imperfection, Indecision and Hoarding." *Current Psychology* 37:445–53.

Ciarrochi, J., A. Bailey, and R. Harris. 2014. *The Weight Escape: Stop Fad Dieting, Start Losing Weight and Reshape Your Life Using Cutting-Edge Psychology*. London: Penguin Viking.

Curran, T., and A. Hill. 2019. "Perfectionism Is Increasing over Time: A Meta-Analysis of Birth Cohort Differences from 1989 to 2016." *Psychological Bulletin* 145(4):410–29.

Deutsch, C. J. 1984. "Self-Reported Sources of Stress among Psychotherapists." *Professional Psychology: Research and Practice* 15(6):833–45.

Egan, S. J., T. Wade, and R. Shafran. 2012. "The Transdiagnostic Process of Perfectionism." *Spanish Journal of Clinical Psychology* 17(3):279–94.

Ellis, A. 2003. "How to Deal with Your Most Difficult Client—You." *Journal of Rational-Emotive and Cognitive-Behavioral Therapy* 21(3/4):203–13.

Ferrari, M., K. Yap, N. Scott, D. A. Einstein, and J. Ciarrochi. 2018. "Self-Compassion Moderates the Perfectionism and Depression Link in Both Adolescence and Adulthood." *PLOS ONE* 13(2):e0192022.

Frost, R., and R. Gross. 1993. "The Hoarding of Possessions." *Behaviour Research and Therapy* 31(4):367–81.

Gilbert, P. 2009. *The Compassionate Mind*. London: Robinson.

Gilbert, P. 2017. "Shame and the Vulnerable Self in Medical Contexts: The Compassionate Solution." *Medical Humanities* 43(4):211–17.

Gilbert, P., K. McEwan, C. Irons, R. Bhundia, R. Christie, C. Broomhead, and H. Rockliff. 2010. "Self-harm in a Mixed Clinical Population: The Roles of Self-Criticism, Shame, and Social Rank." *British Journal of Clinical Psychology* 49(4):563–76.

Hari, J. 2018. *Lost Connections: Why You're Depressed and How to Find Hope.* London: Bloomsbury Publishing.

Hayes, S. 2019. *A Liberated Mind: How to Pivot Toward What Matters.* New York: Avery.

Hayes, S., K. Strosahl, and K. Wilson. 2016. *Acceptance and Commitment Therapy: The Process and Practice of Mindful Change.* New York: The Guilford Press.

Hayes, S., and S. Smith. 2005. *Get Out of Your Mind & Into Your Life.* Oakland, CA: New Harbinger Publications.

Hill, A. P., and T. Curran. 2016. "Multidimensional Perfectionism and Burnout: A Meta-Analysis." *Personality and Social Psychology Review* 20(3):269–88.

Kobori, O., G. Dighton, and R. Hunter. 2020. "Does Perfectionism Impact Adherence to Homework Assignment? A Preliminary Pilot Study of Perfectionism and Procrastination of CBT Homework." *Behavioural and Cognitive Psychotherapy* 48(2):243–47.

Kobori, O., M. Hayakawa, and Y. Tanno. 2009. "Do Perfectionists Raise Their Standards After Success? An Experimental Examination of the Reevaluation of Standard Setting in Perfectionism." *Journal of Behavior Therapy and Experimental Psychiatry* 40(4):515–21.

Kolts, R. 2016. *CFT Made Simple.* Oakland, CA: New Harbinger Publications.

Lee-Baggley, D. 2019. *Healthy Habits Suck: How to Get Off the Couch and Live a Healthy Life... Even if You Don't Want To.* Oakland, CA: New Harbinger Publications.

Leonard-Curtin, A., and T. Leonard-Curtin. 2019. *The Power of Small.* Dublin: Hachette Books Ireland.

Lundh, L. 2004. "Perfectionism and Acceptance." *Journal of Rational-Emotive and Cognitive-Behavior Therapy* 22(4):255–69.

Maslach, C., and M. P. Leiter. 2016. "Understanding the Burnout Experience: Recent Research and Its Implications for Psychiatry." *World Psychiatry* 15(2):103–11.

Moroz, M., and D. M. Dunkley. 2018. "Self-Critical Perfectionism, Experiential Avoidance, and Depressive and Anxious Symptoms over Two Years: A Three-Wave Longitudinal Study." *Behavior Research and Therapy* 112:18–27.

Ong, C. W., J. L. Barney, T. S. Barrett, E. B. Lee, M. E. Levin, and M. P. Twohig. 2019. "The Role of Psychological Inflexibility and Self-Compassion in Acceptance and Commitment Therapy for Clinical Perfectionism." *Journal of Contextual Behavioral Science* 13:7–16.

Ong, C., E. Lee, J. Krafft, C. Terry, T. Barrett, M. Levin, and M. Twohig. 2019. "A Randomized Controlled Trial of Acceptance and Commitment Therapy for Clinical Perfectionism." *Journal of Obsessive-Compulsive and Related Disorders* 22:100444.

Owens, R. G., and P. D. Slade. 2008. "So Perfect It's Positively Harmful? Reflections on the Adaptiveness and Maladaptiveness of Positive and Negative Perfectionism." *Behavior Modification* 32(6):928–937.

Rogers, C. 1961. *On Becoming a Person.* New York: Houghton Mifflin.

Sandoz, E., and T. DuFrene. 2013. *Living with Your Body and Other Things You Hate: How to Let Go of Your Struggle with Body Image Using Acceptance & Commitment Therapy.* Oakland, CA: New Harbinger Publications.

Santanello, A. W., and F. L. Gardner. 2007. "The Role of Experiential Avoidance in the Relationship between Maladaptive Perfectionism and Worry." *Cognitive Therapy and Research* 30(3):319–332.

Sedley, B., and L. Coyne. 2020. *Stuff That's Loud: A Teen's Guide to Unspiraling When OCD Gets Noisy.* Oakland, CA: New Harbinger Publications.

Silberstein-Tirch, L. 2019. *How to Be Nice to Yourself.* Emeryville, CA: Althea Press.

Slade, P. D., and R. G. Owens. 1998. "A Dual Process Model of Perfectionism Based on Reinforcement Theory." *Behavior Modification* 22(3):372–90.

Smith, M. M., D. H. Saklofske, G. Yan, and S. B. Sherry. 2017. "Does Perfectionism Predict Depression, Anxiety, Stress, and Life Satisfaction after Controlling for Neuroticism? A Study of Canadian and Chinese Undergraduates." *Journal of Individual Differences* 38:63–70.

Smith, M., S. Sherry, S. Chen, D. Saklofske, C. Mushquash, G. Flett, and P. Hewitt. 2018. "The Perniciousness of Perfectionism: A Meta-Analytic Review of the Perfectionism–Suicide Relationship." *Journal of Personality* 86(3):522–42.

Stoddard, J. 2019. *Be Mighty: A Woman's Guide to Liberation from Anxiety, Worry & Stress Using Mindfulness and Acceptance.* Oakland, CA: New Harbinger.

Stoddard, J. A., and N. Afari. 2014. *The Big Book of ACT Metaphors.* Oakland, CA: New Harbinger Publications.

Timpano, K., C. Exner, H. Glaesmer, W. Rief, A. Keshaviah, E. Brähler, and S. Wilhelm. 2011. "The Epidemiology of the Proposed DSM-5 Hoarding Disorder: Exploration of the Acquisition Specifier, Associated Features, and Distress." *Journal of Clinical Psychiatry* 72(6):878–90.

Tirch, D., L. R. Silberstein-Tirch, R. T. Codd, M. J. Brock, and M. J. Wright. 2019. *Experiencing ACT from the Inside Out: A Self-Practice/Self-Reflection Workbook for Therapists.* New York: The Guilford Press.

Trub, L., J. Powell, K. Biscardi, and L. Rosenthal. 2018. "'The Good Enough'" Parent: Perfectionism and Relationship Satisfaction Among Parents and Nonparents." *Journal of Family Issues* 39(10):2862–2882.

Twohig, M. P., M. E. Levin, and C. W. Ong. 2021. *ACT in Steps.* Oxford: Oxford University Press.

van den Hout, M., and M. Kindt. 2004. "Obsessive–Compulsive Disorder and the Paradoxical Effects of Perseverative Behaviour on Experienced Uncertainty." *Journal of Behavior Therapy and Experimental Psychiatry* 35(2):165–81.

Walser, R. 2019. *The Heart of ACT: Developing a Flexible, Process-Based, and Client-Centered Practice Using Acceptance and Commitment Therapy.* Oakland, CA: New Harbinger Publications.

Weinberger, A. H., M. Gbedemah, A. M. Martinez, D. Nash, S. Galea, and R. D. Goodwin. 2018. "Trends in Depression Prevalence in the USA from 2005 to 2015: Widening Disparities in Vulnerable Groups." *Psychological Medicine* 48(8):1308–1315.

Welford, M. 2016. *CFT for Dummies.* Chichester, UK: John Wiley & Sons.

White, R.G., P. Larkin, J. McCluskey, J. Lloyd, and H. McLeod. 2020. "The Development of the 'Forms of Responding to Self-Critical Thoughts Scale' (FoReST)." *Journal of Contextual Behavioral Science* 15:20–9.

Wilson, K. G., and A. R. Murrell. 2004. "Values Work in Acceptance and Commitment Therapy: Setting a Course for Behavioral Treatment." In *Mindfulness and Acceptance: Expanding the Cognitive-Behavioral Tradition,* by S. C. Hayes, V. M. Follette, and M. M. Linehan, 120–51. New York: Guilford Press.

Wilson, K. G., and T. DuFrene. 2008. *Mindfulness for Two: An Acceptance and Commitment Therapy Approach to Mindfulness in Psychotherapy.* Oakland, CA: New Harbinger Publications.

Wilson, K., and T. DuFrene. 2012. *The Wisdom to Know the Difference: An Acceptance & Commitment Therapy Workbook for Overcoming Substance Abuse.* Oakland, CA: New Harbinger Publications.

Jennifer Kemp, MPsych, is a clinical psychologist in private practice in Adelaide, South Australia. Kemp works with adults and adolescents on issues such as perfectionism, anxiety, obsessive-compulsive disorder (ODC), eating disorders, and chronic illness. Kemp uses acceptance and commitment therapy (ACT) to help people notice their experiences, make conscious choices "in the moment," and take action toward a fulfilling life.

Foreword writer **Lisa W. Coyne, PhD**, is a licensed clinical psychologist and researcher. She is assistant professor at Harvard Medical School/McLean Hospital in the division of child and adolescent psychiatry, where she specializes in the treatment of anxiety disorders and OCD.

Real change *is* possible

For more than forty-five years, New Harbinger has published proven-effective self-help books and pioneering workbooks to help readers of all ages and backgrounds improve mental health and well-being, and achieve lasting personal growth. In addition, our spirituality books offer profound guidance for deepening awareness and cultivating healing, self-discovery, and fulfillment.

Founded by psychologist Matthew McKay and Patrick Fanning, New Harbinger is proud to be an independent, employee-owned company. Our books reflect our core values of integrity, innovation, commitment, sustainability, compassion, and trust. Written by leaders in the field and recommended by therapists worldwide, New Harbinger books are practical, accessible, and provide real tools for real change.

 **newharbinger**publications

MORE BOOKS from
NEW HARBINGER PUBLICATIONS

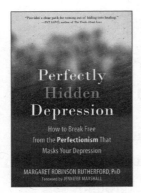